ELEVEN GENETIC GATEWAYS TO SPIRITUAL AWAKENING

ELEVEN GENETIC GATEWAYS TO SPIRITUAL AWAKENING

Leonard Sweet

ABINGDON PRESS
Nashville

ELEVEN GENETIC GATEWAYS TO SPIRITUAL AWAKENING

Copyright © 1998 by Abingdon Press

All rights reserved.

No part of this work may be reproduced or transmitted in any form or by any means, electronic or mechanical, including photocopying and recording, or by any information storage or retrieval system, except as may be expressly permitted by the 1976 Copyright Act or in writing from the publisher. Requests for permission should be addressed in writing to Abingdon Press, 201 Eighth Avenue South, P. O. Box 801, Nashville, TN 37202, U.S.A.

This book is printed on acid-free, recycled paper.

Cataloging-in-publication information is available from the Library of Congress

---

ISBN 0-687-05173-8 (alk. paper)

Education of the National Council of Churches of Christ in the USA. Used by permission.

Quotations noted TANAKH are from *The TANAKH: The New JPS Translation According to the Traditional Hebrew Text*. Copyright © 1985 by the Jewish Publication Society. Used by permission.

The excerpt from *CellChurch* magazine on p. 68 is used by permission.

"The Hot-House" by Robert Minhinnick is used by permission of Seren Books, Ltd.

"East Coker" and "Little Gidding" from *T. S. Eliot: Collected Poems, 1909-1962*; by permission of Harcourt Brace Jovanovich and Faber and Faber.

For
Members of the
Great Books Seminar
(North Indiana Conference)

The Most
Genetically Endowed Leaders I Know

Rachel D. Bales-Case, James W. Beckley, Stephen A. Beutler, Donald W. Brenneman, C. Wesley Brookshire, Stephen Cain, Kaye R. Casterline, Lorin L. Clemenz, Steven K. Conner, Gregory L. Enstrom, Jual H. Evans, Charles E. Gast Jr., Marilyn J. Gebert, Norman R. Glassburn, Stevan R. Haiflich, C. David Hogsett, Charles I. Johnson, Don Johnson, Byron W. Kaiser, Douglas J. Knight, Evan L. Lash, Philip W. Lutz, James D. MacDonald, Jeffrey J. Marshall, David A. Michel, Richard Pickering, Larry M. Ray, Terry C. Rhine, David A. Schrader, Dennis A. Shock, Ronald A. Spyker, Daniel R. Stone, Dean V. Stuckey, Lester L. Taylor, Richard L. Taylor, George Weister, Brian J. Witwer

CONTENTS

ACKNOWLEDGMENTS

"Patriotism," John Hewitt once observed, "has to do with keeping the country in good heart." This book, at the same time the most provincial and the most general book I have written, is dedicated to keeping the church in good heart, both in its Wesleyan particularities and in its larger postmodern manifestations.

But this book could never have been written if certain people didn't keep *me* in "good heart" these past couple of years. The SpiritVenture Ministries (SVM) TeamNet of Aana Lisa Johnson Whatley and Estelle Brendle, headquartered in Charlotte, North Carolina, pulled the ministry out of more bogs and bungles than I care to remember, and in so doing enabled me to function under the lash of a hoard of deadlines while still being available for life. I am grateful for their chastening as well as cheering presence in my life.

Every academic who becomes an administrator is sorry for not having written more. I am no different, but there are people who make me less sorry than I would otherwise be. Thelma Monbarren gave me ten plus, plush years as my administrative assistant. Her successor, Lynn DeBiasse, who puts me to shame in the energy department, suffers from an embarrassment of riches in gifts and graces. There are worse embarrassments.

This entire project would not have been conceived if Kelly Truitt of Wilmington, Delaware, my host for a 1996 renewal weekend at her church, had not insisted on taking me on an unwelcomed jaunt to "Barratt's Chapel." As a dutiful guest I did what was expected—and there experienced the unexpected and conceived this project. I then tested it out on the "Great Books Seminars," one of my most favorite-things-in-life to do. Over ten years ago Elvin Miller, chair of continuing education for the North Indiana Conference, convinced

9

me to invest six days a year in working with a select group of ministers. It was the exuberance of his vision of a new model of continuing formation for clergy that called me forth. I have come back many times to his words spoken in the living room of my Dayton View home, and esteem him as one of the big Barnabas presences in my life. His successors Harold Oechsle (1989–1994) and Susan D. Messenger (1994–present) have developed and deepened his vision, and have created one of the most exciting and cutting-edge conference models of lifelong learning. There is a reason why creative ministry is denser in North Indiana than almost anywhere else in the church today.

Katherine Paterson, author of award-winning children's literature, writes "I love revisions. Where else in life can spilled milk be transformed into ice cream? We cannot go back and revise our lives, but being allowed to go back and revise what we have written comes closest."[1] Historians Philip Lawton and Allen B. Clark are more qualified to write this book than I am. I am grateful to them for their good humor in churning so much skimmed milk. Historian Kenneth Rowe's great erudition and èlan gave this book a lot of whatever creamy taste it has. Research Assistants Linda Martin, Tasha Whitten, and Richard Lambord helped me take such a rapid canter over three hundred years of history, as well as reduced my dizziness from the book's vertiginous leaps forward and back in time.

This is the first book I have finished in ten years that Betty O'Brien hasn't midwifed directly. She still orchestrates delivery from her retirement home in Boulder, Colorado, and since I forgot to thank her in my last book, I need to make some amends here. Betty has been the cause of my life's many foot-in-mouth moments, and the cure of my writings' many tongue-in-cheek blemishes and thumb-in-eye blunders. Betty and I have finally gotten smart: we insist on endnotes since our footnotes can become so copious they muscle the text from the page. Betty understands my passion for finding and documenting the lost detail, the numinous nugget. Wesley's contemporary Henry Fielding said it best: "Love and scandal are the best sweeteners of tea."

In this book I am attempting both to hand over information in familiar form and at the same time to serve it up in new combinations. Hence "NetNotes," which, thanks to Jerome Smith, blurs the line of this "publication" between print and electronics. Since he helped me with this project Jerome has been named Director of Communications for the Southeast Jurisdiction of The United Methodist Church—the first person so hired in the history of our church because of his screen competencies rather than print-based skills. Jerome has always been, will always be, one of those people who make things happen. Southern Baptist pastor Landrum Leavell (Phoenix, Arizona) and Presbyterian pastor Russell E. Mase (Naples, Florida) gave this book a critical scrubbing at the same time they gave me a soul rub.

My motives may be suspected if I heap praise on my boss, Tom Kean, president of United Methodist-related Drew University. If so, then it's just too bad. Governor Kean has been a constant source of encouragement to me personally, and I am grateful. I have learned more about leadership from him than he will ever know.

Life can be grim and grimy, sometimes. But Helen Ewbank of Albion, Michigan knows how to paint the grin on the grim reality underneath. For close to one hundred years she has lived out of these eleven genetic gateways. In her the spirit of the Wesley movement was born. I thank her for showing me how it will be reborn.

Leonard I. Sweet
Christmas Eve, 1997

INTRODUCTION

**You can blow out a candle
But you can't blow out a fire**

Peter Gabriel, "Biko"[1]

Groucho Marx once queried of Chico: "Where are we?" To which Chico replied, "You can't fool me. We're right here!"

So, where are we? Where is "here?"

A television ad for MCI gives us a clue about where "here" is. A child star chants in some of the most profound but creepy words we've heard recently on TV: "There will be a road. It will not connect two points. It will connect all points. It will not go from here to there. There will be no there. We will all only be here."

It's important to know where we are, and how we got there. Let's begin with where we are.

We are living in a marching-off-the-map world.[2] We are living in a Genesis-like world. We are living in a world of such blazing speed that there are more changes in a decade than used to occur in an entire century. We are now living in a world that is almost unrecognizable to our grandparents. Our children will live lives that won't be recognizable to their parents. Two of the biggest companies in the world today, Intel and Microsoft, are built on products that our grandparents couldn't even imagine. One expert predicts that by the year 2000, half the 1995 job descriptions will no longer exist.[3]

No wonder people are having trouble making sense of the world. No wonder people are scared, suspicious, and cynical. Augustine

12

said there was a time when "it was not absolute nothingness. It was a kind of formlessness without any definitions." The postmodern era is that kind of time. The modern era's operator's manual of how to live in the world no longer works. Poet Matthew Arnold expressed our sensation when he observed how people can be "wandering between two worlds, one dead,/The other powerless to be born."[4]

Or in the more contemporary words of the British poet Philip Gross, "How can the centre hold/while maps of half of Europe / hit the shredders?"[5] Novelist Gabriel García Márquez, at the beginning of his *One Hundred Years of Solitude*, writes of a time distant from, yet similar, to ours: "The world was so recent that many things lacked names, and in order to indicate them it was necessary to point."[6]

The Welsh poet/physician Dannie Abse collected five years of his poetry under the title *Ask the Bloody Horse*. Based on Freud's favorite joke about the novice horseman Itzig, Abse prefaces the book with this epigraph: "While Freud was tracing the river to its source he met Itzig riding unsteadily. 'Where are you going?' he asked that wild eyed rider. 'Don't ask me,' said Itzig, 'Ask the bloody horse.'"[7]

Sometimes, from Balaam's ass to Noah's dove to Itzig's horse, our animals know more about where we are headed than we do. But this much we can say: "here" is less boundary than border. Indeed, in the course of each one of our lifetimes we have moved from a world of *boundaries* to a world of *borders*. All over the globe boundaries are coming down, whether boundaries to keep people out (Wall of China) or boundaries to keep people in (Berlin Wall) or boundaries to separate people from one another (the English Channel) or boundaries to distinguish the building from the ground (the continuous systems of movement and materials at the new Guggenheim in Bilbao, Spain).

As the little girl from *The Piano* in that creepy MCI commercial chants, the boundary between "here" and "there" is now virtually gone. We are living in a world where any place can become *every* place. One of the first things I did before taking on my current position was remove the desk from my office and replace it with a conference table. I don't "do desk." If truth be told, I don't even "do office" very well. A virtual office goes with me wherever I go, making the boundaries between being actually present and virtually present smaller and smaller.

13

For Christians, the implications of this shift are as exciting as they are enormous. Boundary ministry/living is different from border ministry/living in transforming ways. In boundaries, life is predictable, controllable, familiar, and well delineated. There are firm conceptual bearings, and one becomes skilled at using categories and concepts that iron out all elements of contradiction, discontinuity, and irrationality from discussions as well as from life.

In borders, life is ill-defined, unformulaic, diffuse, and displaced. There is a sense that the limits are endless while the certainties are nonexistent. Borders have a way of changing and twisting. This is especially so of today's borders, which are like drawing a line in water with your finger. In a world where everyone is a stranger and yet no one is a stranger (in Hebrew the word for "stranger" [zar] is the root of the word "border"—you can't have strangers if you don't have borders), everyday living is anxiety ridden, riddled with uncertainty and often violent. Biblical exegete Darrell Jodock, writing of the scholar's need for battle fatigues while working in these borderlands, writes that "identities now need to be formed amid a prevailing disorientation, a deep existential confusion, and a lack of overarching direction."[8] Fay Weldon's short story "End of the Line" makes the same point through a dizzying assortment of characters and situations, such as Daphne, a lesbian, who wants to become a man, but who lives with Alison, a woman who used to be a man.[9] It takes a computer program to keep track of the characters and situations!

Playwright/politician Vaclav Havel, now president of the Czech Republic, summarized all this in his 4 July 1994 acceptance of the Philadelphia Liberty Medal. The "modern age has ended," he announced. "Today, many things indicate that we are going through a transitional period, when it seems that something is on the way out and something else is painfully being born. It is as if something were crumbling, decaying, and exhausting itself, while something else, still indistinct, were arising from the rubble."[10]

He, like so many of us, calls this new thing "postmodernism." He finds the symbol for what he means by postmodernism in that television ad where a "Bedouin [is] mounted on a camel and clad in traditional robes under which he is wearing jeans, with a transistor radio in his hands and an ad for Coca-Cola on the camel's back."[11]

Can you hear the double ring in Havel's bedouin? Can you see with both eyes the paradoxical combination of future-gazing and

14

retro-grazing that is key to understanding what makes the postmodern world tick and the trick to ministry in Millennium III?

For quite some time I have been arguing that "the postmodernist always rings twice"; that in postmodern culture, we must (in a "both/and" rather than "either/or" fashion) get more ancient and more future at the same time. This book is my attempt to work out this ancient/future methodology in the context of my own tribe, the Wesleyan movement in general and The United Methodist Church in particular. I shall attempt to analyze the Wesleyan movement both in retrospect and in prospect, looking into the past while launching into the future at the same time, functioning as both historian and futurist.

In short, just call me the "repo man" of Methodism. This book is my attempt to repossess the Wesleyan heritage for the new world, to make its soul fresh and singable again among a rising generation, and in a deeper repossession to harness its energies once more for the day in which we live.

I

A Nick Downes cartoon can be awfully funny—literally. One portrays a biblical scene showing a bearded, rough-cut prophet with a stave in his hand turning to answer a crowd following him up a mountain with these words: "Sorry, no. I'm John the Methodist."

I believe that United Methodists don't have to turn people away, or back, or off. We can summon people to join us and follow us into this postmodern future with these words, "Please, yes. I'm Quinn the United Methodist. I'm Courtney the United Methodist. Come on up. Let's cross over to this new world together."

I do not believe my church is a dead-tree tribe. I refuse to join that school of "declinologists" dirging a song of inevitable decline and division that was encapsulated in one recent article entitled "The Demise of the United Methodist Church."[12] I reject the scratch-a-Methodist and find-a-dinosaur attitude so prevalent in sociological circles.

I believe the best days of our tribe, which is moving into its third century as the Christian church is entering its third millennium, lie in front of us, not behind us. I believe God wants to use us as a Noah's

15

dove church that scouts the new world after the boundaries have been washed away, and new borders are evolving, a new vessel that gets to the future first after the sea change and finds the solid ground on which to build new communities of faith.

In fact, God is already up to something in our midst. I see signs of new life and fresh wonders of the Spirit everywhere throughout The U.S.A.'s 294,000 congregations, and especially among the 52,000 congregations that constitute the Wesleyan tribe.

But the choice is ours. Will we, as some say, "rest in peace"? Or will we, once again, "rise in power"? Will it be death or resurrection?

Before a resurrection, however, there must be a burial. We must face the truth about where we are before we can face the truth about where God wants us to be. And the truth of where we are, alas, is this: too much of the church has made Patrick Henry's second choice its first choice—death.

As he lay dying, the French actor Sacha Guitry told a visitor who asked "How are you doing?" "Not as well as yesterday but better than I shall be tomorrow."[13] For my annual conference, West Virginia, that's the way we've had to answer the same question for thirty-four years. We aren't as well as yesterday, but we're better than we shall be tomorrow. We have now logged our thirty-third straight year of membership loss. If absence makes the heart grow fonder, a lot of West Virginia folks love The United Methodist Church.

When the world speaks to us without our being able to speak to it, we are deprived of speech and hence condemned to be untrue.

Colin Morris[14]

The same truth about "absence making the heart grow fonder" could be said for our entire tribe. Who are the biggest religious losers of the twentieth century? The Methodists. We suffered a 48 percent loss in our market share in the past half century.[15] If the chief purpose of a community of faith is to pass on its tradition to its children, we are facing a reproduction crisis of the highest order.[16] The old proph-

16

ecy "the church always stands one generation away from extinction" has almost been self-fulfilled, at least if the recent report by the Office of Research (GCOM) is correct. Called "A Profile of United Methodists Based on the Survey of United Methodist Opinion," it appears that 61.4 percent of us are over fifty (the national average is 25.5 percent); 12.2 percent of us are under thirty-four, and the number of us under thirty is dropping rapidly.[17] Unlike what was supposed to happen, according to a 1987 study conducted by the Hartford Seminary Center for Social and Religious Research, boomers (even the older boomers born between 1946 and 1954) haven't returned to the church although they are, to some degree, "rediscovering religion."[18]

The Welsh poet Robert Minhinnick, in a collection of poems entitled *The Looters*, has a poem with the emboldening title "What's the Point of Being Timid when the House is Falling Down."[19] In no timid terms, a pastor from North Carolina (Don Haynes), after identifying the typical United Methodist congregation as an ocean of whitecaps, suggests that every night all bishops ought to get on their knees and thank God for medical science. Our churches are being kept alive primarily by the ability to prolong human life.

The handwriting is on the wall. Many mainline Protestant churches are broke, or already on financial life-support systems. Some church *buildings* are lucky: endowments keep the empty pews warm, the rooms well-lit, and the roof secure. Lyle Schaller asks "What is the one universal characteristic of every Christian congregation on the North American continent as we prepare for a new millennium?" He answers his own question: "During the next several decades, every member will do one or more of the following: (1) move away or (2) drop out or (3) die."[20] A funeral director in New Jersey told his pastor "I'm going to be seeing a lot more of the congregation than you are in the next few years."

Perhaps we are not so much losing as we are lost. We are like the mother and daughter who visited the Tower of London Museum while traveling in England. The exhibits there are in chronological order, and as they were passing through the medieval armor section, they heard this announcement, so similar to our current predicament, over the speaker system: "Excuse me, ladies and gentlemen, but we have a little American boy lost in the eighteenth century."

We have an entire tribe lost in the 1950s, or more precisely, lost in a world that is no more. We have a church that is stuck doing

17

Industrial Age drills, frozen in models of ministry that no longer work. Consultant/author Herb Miller estimates that fewer than 30 percent of congregations have "moved out of the 1955 patterns that worked so well with the young adults who fought in World War II."[21] Our problems are not unlike those faced by Cadillac, whose average customer a few years ago was sixty-eight, one generation beyond the forty-six-year-old average luxury car owner.[22] The only difference is that Cadillac is now doing better, having turned the boomer corner.

That is why Chico Marx was right. It is imperative we understand the world that is actually "here." For the world that is "here" is hungry for a spiritual awakening.[23] "A "heightened sensitivity" to spiritual concerns and values is a major feature of the shift toward a postmodern outlook, scholars tell us.[24]

Could it be that God wants to work through us what our ancestors called a "heaven sent, Holy Ghost revival," an awakening of the Spirit?

II

Part of the shift from "modern" to "postmodern" is a shift in metaphors from "distinctive culture" or "unique personality traits" to organic systems metaphors. The most important of these—"genes," the "open-sesame" to the Book of Life—comes from the world of molecular biotechnology.

We used to talk about harnessing the power of the atom. Today it is harnessing the power of the genes. Over forty years ago (1953) at Cambridge University, thirty-five year-old Francis Crick and his twenty-four year-old colleague James Watson discovered a double-helical twisted ladder called DNA. Thirteen years later (1966) the genetic code was deciphered, and seven short years later (1973) the rDNA technique was discovered for deleting and recombining genes, and the first gene cloned.[25] On Wednesday morning, 27 September 1995, newspapers around the world announced the "Dawning of the Genetic Age." The announcement was tied to the publication of the Genome Directory by the British science journal *Nature*, and the descent from the mountaintop of the first molecular biologists with peeks into the stone tablets of our species.

For a decade now the most ambitious scientific project in the history of humanity, the Human Genome Project, has been scanning and mapping the human genetic code, the grand total of the genetic information contained in microscopic strands of human DNA. A combined effort of dedicated molecular biology laboratories throughout the world, the multi-billion-dollar Human Genome Project headed by Francis Collins of the National Institutes of Health has now successfully pinpointed, sequenced and published 50 percent of the 3,000,000,000 chemical units/letters in the human genetic code.

As legislated by Congress in 1990, the Human Genome Project has four goals, which will be completed six or seven years before the original target date of 2010: "mapping the twenty-three human chromosomes, sequencing them in their entirety on computer databases, distributing the information freely to scientists throughout the world, and establishing an ethical component to ensure that the knowledge obtained is not used to discriminate against anyone."[26] In the publication of this veritable atlas of ourselves, we've lost our genetic innocence and we can't get it back. "Yesterday's ignorance has been dissipated," writes philosopher Philip Kitcher. Kitcher is not the only one concerned that this tsunami of genetic knowledge, at once as terrifying as it is inspiring, is far surpassing society's ability to deal with this new knowledge wisely.[27]

Genes are the organic, dynamic, and formal organizing elements of the cell, and of the entire organism. Every living cell carries the genetic blueprint of the whole organism. The information encoded in these bundled, twisted ribbons of molecules are called DNA. DNA is a recipe for how each cell in the body should grow, fight off infection, and think. DNA codes are the dynamic software packages supplying rules of interaction and engagement for the body. DNA is a blueprint that tells a protein what to do, making every human body in part an expression of the desires of the exact sequence of the four chemical letters that make up each one of our 100,000 genes.

So you get an idea of just how monumental and how mysterious DNA really is, here are some comparisons:

- If the biochemical instructions for building another you, which is contained in every cell of your body, could be placed into five hundred-page recipe books, it would require more than one thousand volumes.

19

- The simple printing out of the three billion DNA base pairs of a single person's genome would fill thirteen full sets of the *Encyclopaedia Britannica*.[28]
- The genetic instructions for building a human being, the information encoded in one member of *Homo sapiens*, would require roughly 10^{28} kilobytes of storage (that's 1 followed by 28 zeros). By contrast, the total information stored in all the books ever written (estimated at one billion) would require only 10^{12} (or about a million million kilobytes of storage), a mind-boggling difference of 10^{16} (1 followed by 16 zeros).[29]
- If the genetic code is a computer program, the "operating system," for the entire organism, it is some three billion bits long but small enough to fit easily on a CD-ROM.[30]
- The total length of DNA stored in each of your cells is about as long as your arm, three feet of genetic "string." Unravel your body with its trillions of cells like a ball of twine, and there would be enough DNA-string to reach to the moon and back ten thousand times.[31]
- Tinier than the head of a pin, all the DNA of all the humans who ever lived (twenty to thirty billion) would fit into a space tinier than a teardrop.

If the Human Genome Project is the most ambitious scientific research in history (far surpassing the Manhattan Project with which it is often compared), the research into making "molecular computers" out of pieces of DNA is perhaps the most revolutionary. The future is in atoms, not bits—a future that is moving faster and further into the present than previously dreamed possible. Already University of Southern California mathematician Leonard A. Deleman has built out of the genetic material found in the cells of every animal and plant a DNA computer that can solve mathematical puzzles.

It is farmers more than scientists, however, who have been the real pioneers of the Genetic Age. If you ever see a sign that says, "We serve no genetically altered foods," don't believe it. There is hardly a food we eat that hasn't been genetically altered, from hybrid corn or hybrid wheat to the engineered milk of engineered cattle. Within twenty-five years each one of us will have a universal chip (an electronic "smart card") on which will be stored our genetic fingerprint (along with a lot more information like bank accounts, resumé, credit cards, religious preferences) and our personal genomic data.

DNA is what makes us prone to certain diseases. At the point where each of us stands genetically naked, and our potential future health history is readily available, every one of us will realize that we are handicapped—that we have inherited certain flaws and bugs, bad chips, abnormal alleles and viruses. Once again, another boundary will soon fall—the boundary between the "disabled" and the "normal."

In fact, within a decade we will have identified at least one hundred of the genes that predispose us to the almost five thousand genetic diseases, and shortly thereafter will know most of the genes contributing to genetically complex diseases. In what is becoming almost a gene-of-the-month club, scientists are discovering genetic triggers for breast cancer (actually, two breast cancer genes have been located on chromosomes 13 and 17), colon cancer, Alzheimer's disease, hypertension, heart arrhythmia (long QT syndrome), obesity, and so forth.

In *The Lives to Come*, Philip Kitcher warns that popular discussions about genes must bear a disclaimer: "The International Union of Molecular Biologists has determined that casual thinking about genes is likely to cause misguided social policies."[32] Nowhere is this warning more needed than in our coming to terms with what appears to be genetic components to complex human traits like shyness, aggression, alcoholism, criminality, social aberrance, homosexuality, even "novelty seeking,"[33] as well as to such innocuous human characteristics as tongue curling or hair balding. Philosopher Daniel Dennett warns that to find that some physical process or psychological state is attributable to some biological component is not to find for genetic determinism.

With an annual global investment in international bio-development at around eighteen billion U.S. dollars, of which two-thirds come from the private sector and one-third from government, there are some 2,800 companies worldwide that have an interest in gene "pharming."[34] "Genetaceuticals" are treatments combining the best of pharmaceuticals and the best of genetic research. Already the bio-industrial-scientific complex (unofficially dubbed "DNA Incorporated") has developed at least fifty DNA tests for hereditary diseases, including cystic fibrosis, certain kinds of muscular dystrophy, hemophilia, as well as soon to be introduced tests for Alzheimer's disease, breast cancer, manic depression, and certain kinds of colon cancer.[35] In 1994, a gene that keeps cancer from spreading (nm23 on chromosome 6) was discovered by scientists at the University of Pennsylvania. In short, DNA is the future present in the past. While genes can be changed by culture and experience, through DNA the pull of the future is built into every body.

The so-called "world's smartest human," Murray Gell-Mann at California Institute of Technology, puts the pull of DNA in the following gene talk: "In biological evolution, experience of the past is compressed in the genetic message encoded in DNA. In the case of human societies, the schemata are institutions, customs, traditions, and myths. They are, in effect, kinds of cultural DNA."[36]

We are all coded beings. Our bodies are coded; our communities are coded; our churches are coded. We are genetically encoded to think certain ways and do certain things; we are genetically incapable of doing other things. In other words, there is such a thing as ecclesial DNA, bred from the founders, which shapes our basic characteristic as a tribe in the Christian church. Some things are in our genes to do; other things are simply "not in the genes."

This book is an exercise in improving my/our genetic literacy about a spiritual and social movement called "Wesleyanism." It is my attempt at genetic sleuthing of a DNA fingerprint for Methodism in America. It is my attempt as a historian at cracking the genetic code of the Wesleyan movement.

Different cultures are gifted with different DNA. Different cultures obey different codes. What unique strands of DNA are hardwired into the genetic program of our ecclesiastical species? What keys unlock the inner spiritual dynamics of the Wesleyan tradition that made it such a momentous force for God and the gospel? What are the ecclesiastical lineages that have shaped us and continue yet to change over time?

As an exercise in ecclesiastical genetics, or what scholars would call semiotic and mimetic decoding, this endeavor has its limits. We can't read the entire "text" of the Wesleyan genome. It is still being worked out, and what you and I decide to do after reading this book contributes to it. Too much of our history is the story of how the Methodist movement did not live out of its genetic endowments, and failed to sustain its genetic commitments. Race issues, for example, tested Methodist faithfulness to its genetic code virtually every day of its history. Sadly, by and large Methodism failed the tests, and cut against the grain of its lineages. Genetically programmed rightly, Methodism mutated wrongly.

Furthermore, *every* gene code is full of bugs. We are all the products of lotteries, both genetic and environmental, that distribute benefits unequally. While 5 percent of the population is born with genes that make them "uninsurable" without a system of health care, every genome is dogged by at least one bad gene. Abnormal or defective alleles (one of a group of genes) plague every one of our bodies. Philosophical viruses can be found in every social organism. That is why periodically we need to reengineer the genetic coding.

But nothing is more delicate than gene therapy and genetic splicing.[37] Molecular geneticists can create new and better genes by a technique called "recombination." They take existing DNA from a single species, or even from different donor species, and splice together sections of chromosomes into new and better combinations. Bioengineers can even splice human genes into the chromosomes of pigs, sheep, chickens, and goats. In other words, they edit the gene, like a writer edits a sentence, to make it work better. In this way organisms are given new cells which make them resistant to disease, or even help in combating disease. Far from genetic engineering being something novel in nature, Lynn Margulis has shown how humans are only now adopting techniques pioneered and practiced by prokaryotes for billions of years.

Although I am convinced that at certain points the Wesleyan organism could use some "recombination" to address its defective alleles, I will leave it to another essay to discuss how the Wesleyan movement needs to be a recombinant faith community. Suffice it here to say that while we need to be a learning organism, we also need to be an unlearning organism. No genome hasn't "learned" some things that aren't any longer a reflection of reality. Environmental modulation of genetic predispositions is crucial to the survival of any species.

III

To crack the genetic code of Wesleyanism, we need to go prospecting for the future in the past. What would we discover if we took

23

a pilgrimage to the place known as the "Cradle of Methodism," and there rock the cradle of our church?

T. S. Eliot begins "East Coker" advocating this methodology of going "back to the future:"

"In my beginning is my end . . ."

In "Little Gidding" Eliot writes "What we call the beginning is often the end/And to make an end is to make a beginning." The end of all our exploration, he hastens to add, "Will be to arrive where we started/And know the place for the first time."[38]

The beginning of the Wesleyan movement in America, the place where we started, is called Barratt's Chapel in Frederica, Delaware. The chapel, now designated a Methodist Historic Shrine, was built by Phillip Barratt, the sheriff of Kent County and member of the General Assembly, who was converted to Christ under the preaching of Freeborn Garrettson. Barratt died at the age of fifty-five, two weeks before the historic meeting on 14 November 1784.

One of the most historic buildings of American Methodism (the third oldest Methodist church edifice in the world and the oldest surviving church in the U.S. built for and by Methodists), Barratt's Chapel is known as the "Cradle of Methodism."

Let all preaching houses be built plain and decent; but not more expensive than is absolutely unavoidable: Otherwise the necessity of raising money will make rich men necessary to us. But if so, we must be dependent upon them, yea and governed by them. And then farewell to the Methodist discipline, if not doctrine too.

John Wesley[39]

At the close of the Revolutionary War, John Wesley sent to America his chief lieutenant in England, Ireland, and Wales, Thomas Coke LL.D. of Jesus College, Oxford. Ordained in the Church of England, Coke helped Wesley ordain Richard Whatcoat and Thomas Vasey on

2 September 1784, before Wesley sent Coke and the others across the Atlantic with these specific instructions: Find Francis Asbury, Methodism's George Washington, and together work out and superintend the future of American Methodism.

The first bishop of the Methodist Episcopal Church in America, Thomas Coke landed in New York on 3 November. Eleven days later (14 November 1784) Coke arrived at Barratt's Chapel, where he was invited to preach. Francis Asbury arrived during the sermon. After Coke had finished preaching, Asbury stepped forward and Coke stepped down from the pulpit. There they met and embraced.

After the service, Asbury and Coke and twelve other preachers met at the home of Barratt's widow, Miriam Sipple, where they got to know one another, resolved their differences, and began implementing Wesley's plan for the American Methodist churches, although with a difference. Asbury refused Wesley's appointment as "superintendent" (later called "bishop") unless elected democratically by his colleagues and assisted in the ordination service by his friend William Otterbein, later co-founder of the Church of the United Brethren in Christ.

In America there are [no bishops], neither any parish ministers. So that for some hundred miles together, there is none either to baptize or to administer the Lord's Supper. . . . I conceive myself at full liberty . . . by appointing and sending labourers into the harvest.

I have accordingly appointed Dr. Coke and Mr. Francis Asbury to be joint superintendents over our brethren in North America. . . . And I have prepared a liturgy little differing from that of the Church of England. . . . I also advise the elders to administer the Supper of the Lord on every Lord's Day.

John Wesley on the "emergency"
situation after the American Revolution[40]

25

It was at Barratt's Chapel where the Methodist movement in America "cut the umbilical cord from its Anglican mother," in the words of the University of Delaware historian William Williams, who knows more about this episode than perhaps anyone alive today. Barratt's Chapel was the Methodist movement in America's "Declaration of Independence."

Here is where Coke and Asbury implemented Wesley's plans for the Methodist Episcopal Church of America. Here is where Asbury and Coke planned the organizing conference of the Methodist Episcopal Church in America, and assigned Freeborn Garretson the responsibility of gathering the preachers together at Lovely Lane Chapel in Baltimore during the Christmas season. Here is where the hands of American Methodist preachers first officially served the sacraments—both communion and baptism.

Here is where American Methodists exploded from the starting gate of several hundred members in the 1770s to an unheard of 250,000 members in 1820. When in 1773 Thomas Rankin called all the Methodist preachers in America to gather at St. George's Church, Philadelphia, ten showed up. They represented a total membership of 1,160.

Here is where the Wesleyan genogram should be found in its original complexion and complexity.[41]

Here is where we begin to let heritage leverage us into the future.

Here is where we usher in the Millennium III, Century 21 church.

Can The United Methodist Church make the shift from a modern to a postmodern church? It will not be easy. The complexity of the coordinate pluses and losses, gains and pains, makes the transition difficult. But these eleven genetic gateways into the future are a right place to begin.

NetNotes

http://www.leonardsweet.com/netbooks/gateways/

The Netbook Companion for *Eleven Genetic Gateways to Spiritual Awakening* is an Internet guide that allows the reader to go beyond the printed page. At the end of each chapter you will find NetNotes, which give a summary of what you will find on the companion website at http://www.leonardsweet.com/netbooks/gateways/. It contains links, images (a Java-powered slide show is also available on the website), audio, interactive tools, "Rock the Cradle Discussion Questions and Genogram Exercises" and resources from each chapter.

The Gateways Forum is a place to post your chapter-theme related notes for others in an online dialogue. Here you can post ideas and respond to book related themes. Keep in mind that what you post will become a part of the greater scope of the book, which you help become a living book.

The Gateways Guestbook is where you can post your contact and comment information. It is based on the traditional Internet guestbook format: a place for your name, email and other information to be posted. This will allow you to contact others who are involved in the book.

Rock-the-Cradle Discussion Questions and Genogram Exercises

1. Andre Malraux is quoted as saying that "The third millennium must be a spiritual millennium or there will be no third millennium." Would you agree or disagree with this statement? How would you define "spiritual"?

2. Is your church now doing boundary ministry or border ministry? If you were to shift from boundary living to border living, what would the difference mean in the life of your church? For you personally, is the comfort level higher in border ministry or boundary ministry? Which is it for your church?

3. Discuss this declaration by Dean M. Douglas Meeks: "Things are changing in the Methodist household. . . . In the midst of the change we should be aware that God is a strange housebuilder of a strange house. It is a resurrection household that God is struggling to build, a household in which we shall all be able to dance, without our inhibitions and our stiff joints. But God will call the tune. In the resurrection household all the household rules get changed."[42]

4. Wesley's number one fear was this: "I am not afraid that the people called Methodists should ever cease to exist either in

27

Europe or America. But I am afraid lest they should only exist as a dead sect, having the form of religion without the power."[43] Has Wesley's worst nightmare come true?

5. Blockbuster claims to have an outlet within ten minutes of virtually every community in the U.S. Similar claims used to be made by Methodist churches. In an electronic world where any place can become every place, how important is it for us to be planting new churches wherever the people are? Or do "high-tech" and "high-touch" really go together?

6. Have some fun: How would you identify the Jesus genes?

7. Now get serious: When is the last time you discussed the ethical implications of medical scientists developing cloning techniques, genetic screening, using fetal tissue for disease prevention, shifting genes across species barriers? Have you considered what it means that the genomic industry has targeted as "geno-pigs" the most remote, indigenous populations in the far ends of the Earth where cures for asthma, diabetes, and a whole host of other ailments supposedly reside? How do you react to the knowledge that human DNA strands are already being patented by the government and numerous pharmaceutical companies? As of 1995 the United States Patent and Trademark Office has patented human cells, cell lines, viruses, genes, seven animals, and numerous altered plants and micro-organisms. Patents are pending for more than two hundred other genetically engineered animals. Why hasn't any of this drawn the fire and ire of America's religious leaders (that means *you*)?

The Human Genome Project has allocated over 3 percent of its budget to the Ethical, Legal, and Social Implications Branch (ELSI) under the leadership of Nancy Wexler of the Hereditary Disease Foundation. ELSI's four areas of study are 1) fairness: nondiscriminatory access to genetic information; 2) privacy: rights of individuals to protect themselves against genetic disclosure; 3) delivery systems: fair and equal access to genetic services; 4) education: raising of public consciousness about the new biology.

Do you find this too little, too late? Or do you find this encouraging? Do you agree with the priorities of the ethical guidelines for study established by ELSI?

8. If genetic engineering is not to be used for selfish or destructive ends, how can it serve the needs of the sick, the poor, the weak?

What human disorders might be ethically "correct" through genetic engineering? Down's syndrome? Are all fetal abnormalities "defects?" Theodore Roszak argues that "The Human Genome Project promises the possibility of deleting all hereditary diseases and many constitutional weaknesses from our DNA—or at the very least offering the chance to abort any pregnancy that might produce a less than long-lived specimen."[44] Do you think he's right? Do you think this use of genetic engineering is right?

9. Discuss the theological implications of the following scenario, as presented by Harvey Lodish of the Whitehead Institute for Biomedical Research, who believes that soon and very soon computers will "screen" a fetus and monitor its health from the inputting of human DNA information and the mother's medical history.

> The output will be a color movie in which the embryo develops into a fetus, is born, and then develops into an adult, explicitly depicting body size and shape, hair, skin and eye color. Eventually the DNA sequence base will be expanded to cover genes important for their traits such as speech and musical ability; the mother will be able to hear the embryo as an adult speak or sing.[45]

10. Find out who in your area offers pastoral genetic counseling.

11. A company in Seattle will preserve a person's complete DNA in a glass capsule. Would you subscribe to their services? Why or why not?

12. In an experiment known as "the human-hamster hybrid system," scientists tried to fertilize the ovum of a hamster with the sperm of a male human being, the resulting life-form promising to be something between less than a human being but more than a hamster.[46] Should genetic experimentation with life and such life forms be tolerated? Is this kind of biotechnology defacing the image of God?

13. If you doubt whether genetics is confronting us with choices that require wisdom that is beyond what we have exercised in the past, consider these two ethical dilemmas that are current possibilities. 1) Should parents who have children that are shorter than they would like use growth hormones, even when there is no growth hormone deficiency? 2) Should parents whose children are less intelligent than they would like, or even learning dis-

29

abled, use genetic technology to enhance IQ and mental capacity?

14. If you have access to the Internet you can learn more about Barratt's Chapel by visiting its Web Page and using the following WWW address: http://users.aol.com/Barratts/home.html. Phil Lawton is Pagemaster.

15. Visit Barratt's Chapel, which is owned and maintained by the Commission on Archives and History of the Peninsula Delaware Annual Conference of The United Methodist Church. It is open from 1:30 to 4:30 p.m. Saturdays and Sundays, or by special arrangement with the curator. To schedule tours or make appointments to do research, call 302–335–5544 or write Lynn Hobbs, curator, 6362 Bay Road, Frederica, DE 19946.

16. For the reproduction crisis of the mainline church, read my essay "The Ladder and the Cross: The Plover Report" (see note 16 above).

17. Barratt's Chapel has been in serious need of repairs and ongoing maintenance. The problem became so serious that it was closed during the summer of 1996 for restoration woork. Why not make a contribution, or sponsor a fund-raising event, for the building of an endowment fund for the Cradle of Methodism? Send your contribution to Barratt's Chapel, 6362 Bay Road, Frederica, DE, 19946.

ELEVEN

The TIMING Gene

To serve the present age,
my calling to fulfill
O may it all my powers engage
to do my Master's will.

Charles Wesley[1]

A while back a *New Yorker* cartoon presented the following scene: "This morning opportunity knocked at my door! But by the time I pushed back the bolt, turned the two locks, unlatched the chain, and shut off the alarm system, it was gone."

"TIMING IS EVERYTHING" blares the ad. Well, if not "everything," timing is more than something. In fact, in a postmodern world, timing can be almost as important as content. Whereas today the church's timing is off, our Wesleyan forebears (like the tribe of Issachar) "knew the times" and "knew what to do."[2]

Jesus' keen sense of timing was one key to his ministry. His sense of timing was superb not because he focused on timing itself, but because he focused on the doing of ministry in the time in which God had given him—and the timing took care of itself.

Jesus exquisitely timed everything he did. Jesus could dance without watching his feet because he remained open to the magic of the moment. He knew when to step forward and lead, and when to slip away. He knew when to reveal certain things, and when not to. He knew there were times to fast, and times to feast. There was a time to be protective of his own energies, and a time to share. "My time is

31

not yet come" (John 7:6), he said. But then in John 17:1 we have these words: "The hour is come." And later in the Scriptures: "Now is the accepted time" (2 Corinthians 6:2 KJV).

Do not squander time, for that is the stuff life is made of.

Benjamin Franklin

Jesus trained his disciples not only to cast their nets from the other side, but to know when to pull the net. He wept when his own people "did not recognize the time of your visitation from God," or as another translation puts it, "You did not recognize God's moment when it came" (Luke 19:44 NEB). He called us to read the signs of the times, to be open to what time we had. Jesus assumed we could read the rhythms and rhymes of nature, the "signs of the sky." He challenged his disciples also to know the "signs of the times." When asked to say who he was, Jesus is alleged to have answered: "You test the face of the sky and of the earth, and him who is before your face you have not known, and you do not know to test this moment."[3]

There always comes a moment in time when a door opens and lets the future in.

Graham Greene

One reason we need a heightened sense of timing is because the Devil also boasts a sharp sense of timing. When Satan fails to defeat Jesus in the desert, he withdraws "until an opportune time" (Luke 4:13). That "opportune time" returned at the Mount of Olives. Vacillation, equivocation, tergiversation play into the quick hands of the evil one.

Every United Methodist minister at ordination is admonished "Never trifle away time."[4] The issue of "trifling away time" is at the heart of ministry. Time so mattered to John Wesley that he had a bookshelf installed in his traveling coach so he could make the best possible use of his time.[5] The church needs ministries that are "timely," ministers who will understand that "timeliness" may be as next to godliness as "cleanliness." Church advisor William Easum argues that "when people are hurting, they cannot wait for the church to respond when it wants. When they want to know more about faith, they cannot wait for us to get around to them. When they need someone to listen to them, they do not have time to wait until we are free."[6]

Easum suggests this motto for the postmodern, "permission-giving" church: "any time, any place, for any one, no matter what." To the question "How long is too long?" Easum gets specific: if it takes your church more than ten minutes to decide if the church needs a fax machine, or six months to decide whether to start another worship service, you are "trifling away time."[7]

Timing is important in our everyday life, from cooking an ambitious French meal to taking in a leisurely movie. Not too long ago I was doing a "retreat" (rather an advance, I hope) at the South Central Jurisdiction Retreat Center at Mt. Sequoia in Fayetteville, Arkansas. As part of the discussion of "postmodern," we decided to go see one of the two Quentin Tarantino films of 1994. In classic postmodern fashion, Tarantino was responsible for what may have been the "best" and "worst" films of 1994—*Pulp Fiction* (the "best") and *Natural Born Killers* (the "worst"—Tarantino himself requested that his name be removed from the movie even though he wrote the screenplay for it).

The wrong decision at the wrong time = disaster.
The wrong decision at the right time = a mistake.
The right decision at the wrong time = unacceptance.
The right decision at the right time = success.

John Maxwell[8]

The movie was scheduled to start at 7 p.m. We got there thirty-five minutes early. No one was at the window. It was raining heavily. After waiting in our cars for about ten minutes, we saw movement at the window. We all proceeded to brave the rain and buy our tickets—which the cashier wouldn't sell to us because the ticket window didn't officially open until fifteen minutes before showtime.

Asking if we could wait inside with some popcorn and Coke, we were told that the snack counter didn't open until fifteen minutes before the show. So we all grumpily returned to the rain and our cars, frustrated, feeling awkward, and out-of-sorts.

What would have happened if we had gotten to the movie thirty-five minutes late? The same thing. No one would have known what to do with us. If they had consented to sell us a ticket, we would not have had the time to get popcorn and Coke; we would have disrupted the theater crowd who were well into their movie by then; we would have had to stumble in the dark and take whatever seats were left; we would have missed much of the movie.

Arrive at the movies ten minutes early, and there is exactly the amount of time you need to buy your tickets, get some refreshments, find a good seat. If your timing is really on, as soon as you plop into your seat, the lights go down and the best part of many movies, the previews, begin.

You gotta know when to hold 'em . . .

Kenny Rogers

"Timing is everything" every day. Ideas before their time, or inventions used outside their place, avail nothing. The point is to be punctual: get there ahead of your time, and people can't understand or comprehend what you're doing. Get there too late, and you're behind the times.

In the early nineteenth century Robert Owen, a British industrialist, advocated child labor laws, universal education, shorter work weeks, and other social reforms. People thought he was crazy. It took over a century for his views to be adopted.

Guglielmo Marconi, the inventor of radio, announced to his friends that he was convinced invisible waves could travel through space for great distances and carry information. His "friends" got together and committed him to an insane asylum for a while.

Meanwhile redeem the time, catch the golden moments as they fly.

John Wesley[9]

Charles Babbage worked out on paper history's first calculator and first computer. But he was frustrated in producing them because the technical ability was lacking . . . in 1823.

An Italian priest Giovanni Caselli developed the first commercial fax system between Paris and Lyons . . . in 1865. He called it the pantelegraph—but nobody got it. Nobody used it. So it sat there for a century, waiting for the world to catch up.

Xerox developed the computer mouse . . . fifteen years too soon. It sat on the shelf waiting for a market. Apple took it and made it immensely popular.

Cecile Andrews, the director of continuing education at a Seattle community college, offered a workshop on voluntary simplicity in 1989. Only four people showed up. The course was canceled. In early 1992, she tried once more to interest people in simplicity circles. This time 175 men and women crowded the auditorium.

I

America's challenge in the 1990s is to mount the political equivalent of a revolution to revitalize its institutions. Some such effort will occur. The scope may be sufficient, although more probably it will fall short. But for several reasons, the 1990s are the decade in which to try.[10]

With these words one of America's most respected political commentators, Kevin Phillips, throws down the gauntlet. There is something destabilizing about history's giddy end-decades and turn of centuries that makes people open to thinking and talking about the future, that makes them more aware of discontinuity and thus more accepting of radical change. In other words, if you can't "do it" when a century ends, not to speak of a millennium, you can't "do it" period. Failure to seize this Century 21, Millennium III moment bespeaks a larger failure of leadership.

God's time is always the best time.

John Wesley[11]

Tom Paine called the 1790s "the times that try men's souls." Phillips argues that all 90s are soul-trying times. While end-of-the-century decades have often been pivotal (think of the 1490s, the 1590s, the 1690s, the 1790s?), Phillips isolates a special American tradition of a radical nineties that has given us everything from Jeffersonian populists (1790s) to suffrage extension, referendum, recall, and the People's Party (1890s) to Ross Perot's electronic town hall (1990s).

> The nineties have been prime periods of American political and ideological revolution, as opposed to physical and military upheaval. The 1790s, which began with the essentially conservative triumph of the Constitution and its ratification, finished with something very different: the renewal of anti-elite politics, the election of Thomas Jefferson, and the "Revolution of 1800." A century later, the 1890s, which began with robber-baron capitalism and laissez-faire at its zenith, ended with populism and progressivism on the rise, with William Jennings Bryan barely defeated, with ideas like popular ballot initiatives and direct election of U.S. senators about to spread like a prairie fire.[12]

Analogies help organize questions and isolate possibilities, but they can't predict. Nevertheless, every decade of the nineties in American politics has been a populist decade of redesign and regrouping around the founding ideals of 1776. In the 1790s, again in the 1890s, and most recently in the 1990s, there have been strategic shifts to bring the government closer to the people.

36

What the last decade is to a century the last century is to a millennium.

Atlantic Monthly (1891)[13]

What Phillips failed to see in his insightful probings of the analogies of American politics[14] is that in each of these two earlier nineties decades the Methodists led the way in championing and channeling the people's energies into a spiritual awakening. Evangelicals claimed the vision of a democratized social order and the power of grassroots spirituality. Evangelicals could reinvent themselves in each of the nineties decades partly because Wesley's theology of time related both to one's personal life and also to one's personal place in the stream of history.

Historian Kenneth Rowe puts it like this: "For three centuries in a row, at century's end Methodism has been in disarray, only to renew herself. Only this time it seems to be taking a little longer."[15] In the 1780s-90s, the transition was from a renewal movement to a church. The Methodists stepped into the 1790s as little more than a hiccup in history, and walked into the new century at the very heart of a people's movement that would issue in America's Second Great Awakening. The market share for Methodists was 2.5 percent in 1776. By 1850, the "upstart" Methodists boasted a 34.2 percent share of religious adherence.[16] Methodism had grown from nothing to the largest single religious force in America, with more Methodist churches in the country than post offices.

We don't get to choose our own century, . . . In our hands our time is read.

St. Petersburg poet Aleksandr Kushner[17]

37

The situation one hundred years ago was remarkably similar to now. In the 1890s, America was unsure, unraveling, up-in-the-air, "at sixes and sevens," and vital. It was a time of massive economic transitions (from farm to industrial, from rural to urban), divisive culture wars, dizzying technological advances, destabilizing immigrations. In the 1880s-90s, the transition was from a backstreets church to a Main Street church—with parsonages and residential clergy, with theological seminaries and professional clergy, with official boards and agencies and program ministries. Methodism reinvented itself as a program church, and the church of Bishop Matthew Simpson and Alpha J. Kynett was totally different from the church of Bishop Francis Asbury and Nathan Bangs.

Methodism's timely response to the social ferment of the nineties, and its own version of the dream of democratizing economic power and decentralizing vested power, carried with it the prospect of going too far. In the 1790s there was the possibility of an over identification with American democracy,[18] and the "democratic" Methodists like the Republican Methodists, the Reformed Methodists, and the Protestant Methodists were kicked out as Methodism opted for a democratic gospel but an autocratic polity. This over-response of the 1790s is still with us today in the conflation of church religion and civil religion.

Time is a sacrament of eternity.

P. T. Forsythe

In the 1890s there was the possibility of the embrace of the social gospel as the whole gospel. When the church succeeded in getting the government involved in social justice through Franklin Delano Roosevelt's "New Deal" and Lyndon Johnson's "Great Society," there followed a loss of outward mission and a feeling of superfluousness that is still with us. That is why we need a strong sense of identity that can take us through each nineties period without loss of soul.

The question facing the church at the end of the 1990s is the same one that faced our ancestors in previous century turnings: Will we claim this moment for Christ? Or will we let it pass?

The time is short. In his *Comic Dictionary*, Evan Esar defines the future as "the hereafter which grows shorter everyday of one's life, unlike the past which grows longer."[19] No reading of the times that gives hope would argue otherwise: the church needs fleet-footed ministries. In the past, leaders were those who could execute a task the fastest. Tomorrow's leaders are those who can learn new things the fastest. We need to be quick enough off our feet, and strong enough on our feet, so that we can plunge through the windows of opportunity that literally pass by, windows that God seldom outlines in neon lights.

"Now is the accepted time!" "Now is the day of salvation." Nehemiah knew the time was short, and the opportunity to rebuild the wall of Jerusalem might not come again. So he accomplished the impossible in fifty-two days (Nehemiah 6:15). In the words of Ferdinand Foch: "The most powerful weapon on earth is the human soul on fire."

"Your time is now."

Jesus (John 7:6b)

This is the time for which you and I were born. Our ancestors lived out of the intensity and integrity of the moment. So must we. Our forebears in the faith exuded such passion they turned this culture upside down. So must we. In the words of an anonymous nineteenth-century poem:

The restless millions want the light
Whose coming maketh all things new,
Christ also waits, but men are slow and late;
Have we done what we could? Have I? Have you?

39

NetNotes

http://www.leonardsweet.com/netbooks /gateways/

Here you will find links to *New Yorker* magazine, Ben Franklin, Bill Easum, *Pulp Fiction*, Thomas Paine, John Wesley, Second Great Awakening, Francis Asbury, the Vatican and various timing URL's. The Interactive page allows you to calculate the Life Counter Game. Listen to "God of Grace and God of Glory" and other time related midi files. Selected images include Barratt's Chapel historic marker and other time-related images. Your answers and comments about the "Rock-the-Cradle Discussion Questions and Genogram Exercises" can be posted on the Gateways Forum under the Timing Listing. The resources listing includes all indexed notes from the chapter, plus you can post additional resources under the Gateways Forum Timing Listing.

Rock-the-Cradle Discussion Questions and Genogram Exercises

1. Sing the Harry Emerson Fosdick hymn "God of Grace and God of Glory" and discuss the second stanza which begins: "Lo! the hosts of evil round us / scorn thy Christ, assail his ways!"[20]
2. It has been said "The difference between a hero and a coward is one step sideways." What do you think? What about "The difference between a leader and a martyr is three paces"?
3. If now is your time, what are you being called to do? How is God calling you to "lead?"
4. What is the danger in today's timely response? (Radical relativism?)
5. Pope John Paul II was so aware of his times, and so concerned about timing, that he postponed his coronation until noon so as not to interfere with a scheduled morning soccer match. Where in your church do you need a better sense of timing?
6. Donald J. Shelby, Senior Pastor at the Santa Monica United Methodist Church in Santa Monica, California, received this note from a member of his congregation, now working in Washington, D.C., shortly after Christmas. Have copies of this letter made and give it to each member of the class. Ask them to meditate and pray on it, and then relate how it impacts their soul.

Dear Don:

I am writing this to you because I need to share it, and I believe you will understand.

Jesus came to me last week and I turned away from Him. It was two days before Christmas. I had been working 16 to 18 hours a day and had nothing to prepare for Christmas. I went out in the early afternoon to pick up a couple of gifts. I was wearing a down coat I bought in California, but had just purchased a new one and I wanted to give this coat away. It had been on my mind all day.

I walked out of a book store and within half a block I saw a woman holding out a paper cup, begging for money. I looked in my purse to give her a dollar but all I had were two twenties, and of course I *couldn't* give her that much. So I emptied my change purse into the cup. Two dimes fell on the sidewalk and when I knelt to pick them up, I saw that she was only wearing house slippers. The wind had picked up, it had rained earlier in the day and was very cold. She said to me that she was cold, her jacket was wet and asked me to feel it. I did, but my eyes were still blind. I walked away! I was embarrassed at the thought of giving her my coat, of taking it off there along the street and handing it to her. I had not gotten to the corner before I realized what was happening. I removed my keys from the pocket of the coat and turned back, but she was gone. Usually the street people stay in one place most of the day, and I couldn't believe she was gone in less than one minute. I walked around the block looking for her, then walked another block in each direction, but could not find her. I am still looking each time I go out, but I probably will never see her again. I believe it was Christ in that woman asking for my coat, and I had all kinds of excuses not to give it to her. Please tell everyone, Don, to answer when the Spirit calls, to follow Jesus when He appears to us in the needs of another human being.

I hope I have another chance and I pray I will answer 'Yes.'"[21]

TEN

The *FAST LEARNING/ UNLEARNING* Gene

Unite the pair so long disjoin'd,
Knowledge and vital piety;
Learning and holiness combin'd,
And truth and love let all men see.

Charles Wesley[1]

Fast Learning is key to a spiritual awakening.[2] From the very beginning, the Wesleyan movement touted a singular formula that rocked the religious, social, and political world of its day. In a striking way this formula was a spiritual variant of the physical equation that helped launch the postmodern world.

According to Albert Einstein, the formula that unlocks the secrets to the physical universe is $e=mc^2$ where "e" is energy, "m" is mass, and the constant "c" is the speed of light. Energy and mass are identical when there is a conditional factor present, the speed of light. Light rays are the needles that thread together space and time. Or as physicists like to put it, energy and mass are essentially identical but existentially different.

According to the Wesleys, the formula that unlocks the secrets to the spiritual universe is as follows: knowledge when multiplied by vital piety yields an awakened church. Or expressed as a spiritual equation, $e=mc^3$ where "e" is the energy explosion of an evangelistic awakening, "m" is the mass density of information and maturity of knowledge about the Word and the world, the source of well-being for the church, and "c" cubed is the light of a Christ consciousness raised into three dimensions, each one building exponentially on the other: the depth of a heartfelt faith (the personal dimension), the height of a Christbody community (the communal dimension), and the breadth of a transforming mission (the social dimension).[3] It was the implementation of this spiritual equation that released one of the greatest spiritual awakenings in the history of this planet.

The cubing of a Christ consciousness without the maturity of knowledge is a fire without a fireplace. Wesley believed it took brainpower to do effective ministry, and the Methodist movement invested heavily in intellectual capital. Put it this way: the Methodist movement was born in a learning setting (Oxford University). It will be born again in learning settings as well (church seminaries).

I

We often forget that Wesley himself was a formidable Oxford don, doughty to such a point he supposedly refused to enter the university town of Cambridge, England, because he did not want to lower his academic standards. Wesley believed with Augustine that the best knowledge outside of Christ must be brought together with the best knowledge inside of Christ.

One of the first things American Methodists worried about was education. Barratt's Chapel is where Asbury and Coke laid out the plans for the first Methodist school. Wesley had already demonstrated through the Kingswood School his commitment to education wherever he was ministering, even among the migrant coal miners of Bristol. Hence Asbury's and Coke's concern for a learning center was in keeping with British Methodist genes.

[Asbury] and I have agreed to use our joint endeavours to establish a School or College on the plan of Kingswood-School.

Thomas Coke[4]

43

A month later, Asbury and Coke met and emptied their pockets. Between them they had raised one thousand pounds sterling for this new movement's new school. (How many of us would even have finished our feasibility study?) Within a year, Bishop Asbury spoke at Abingdon, Maryland on the occasion of the cornerstone laying of U.S. Methodists' first Methodist educational center. Its name? Cokesbury, after the two bishops. More than the members of almost any other denomination, Methodists founded schools, colleges, and universities wherever they went.

A learned ministry has been and always will be the key to Methodism's future. It's time to stop talking about education and start talking about learning. Learning encompasses "anytime, anywhere, anybody, anything" in Bill Johnson's 1987 words that bannered Digital Equipment Corporation's networking revolution.

In fact, according to the Wesleyan formula, learning may be more central to a spiritual awakening than worship. Wesley stressed substantive teaching and preaching over pandering to new members. After all, he called his meetings "classes." The early Wesleyans were more concerned about how to send people out rather than how to seduce them in. If our churches were sending out educated disciples, they wouldn't have to worry about bringing in new people to worship. Instead of peopling buildings, our genes tell us to be building people. Instead of making programs, it is in our genes to make disciples.

They know enough who know how to learn.
American historian Henry Adams

In one way, the learning gene shifts the church's focus from "church growth" to "church health." There are a lot of bad ways to produce good numbers. After all, Jesus never did say "Count my Sheep" but "Feed my Sheep." Jesus did not "grow" a mega-church, or even a mega-following. After three years of intensive ministry, he could claim an intimate group of eleven key associates (he lost eight percent of his disciples), and at most one hundred followers. He spent his time, not founding local communities, but training a hand-ful of itinerant disciples in first-century Palestine.

But it was this small band of believers that turned the world upside down and inside out and topsy-turvy.

Herein lies our problem. We have ceased being disciple-making churches. Church advisor/author William Easum contends that our churches are geared up more to make decisions than to make disci-ples.[5] Biblical scholar/Yale professor Leander E. Keck critiques main-line churches, who, "despite their ample theological heritage, are no longer seriously teaching the theological substance of Christian faith. Repeatedly they have abandoned opportunities to ground people more deeply in the faith."[6]

II

The church's educational system is a scandal for a variety of reasons. First, we must free it from the nod-to-God-hour syndrome. "Sunday schools" started off in the late eighteenth century as real "schools" that educated the neediest sectors of society in the use of cutting edge technologies of the day—the books, pamphlets, paper, and writing utensils of print culture—while at the same time educat-ing the masses in the Christian faith. Sunday schools taught illiterate children that "there's gold in them there books."

The importance of Sunday schools in the Victorian church for raising up educated disciples who followed Jesus without counting the cost, without looking back, without saying "never," cannot be overly stressed. Sunday school faculties in the nineteenth century asked for, and got, 50 percent of church floor space, and many Sunday schools grew faster and bigger than churches themselves. Some church leaders opposed Sunday schools for precisely this reason, attacking them as a "competitor to the church," and opposing their separate funding base.[7] Sunday schools were both an engine of evangelism and a vehicle of higher and deeper discipleship. The public school system grew out of the Sunday school movement's market-quality instructional resources and activities.

Knute Larson's success exemplified in his *Growing Adults on Sunday Morning* demonstrates that the church should not throw away this valuable hour on Sunday morning.[8] But "Sunday schools" today are less "schools" than nod-to-God hours. To say that "the theological substance of Christian faith" is being transmitted today from generation to generation through the Sunday school would be a stretch of herculean, even humorous proportions.[9]

Second, we must free the church's educational system from the "lecture-drill-test" methods of the factory model. Religious learning systems must be based on new academic paradigms that shift from passive learning modes to active learning modes, especially ones where students learn habits of the mind and habits of the soul at their own rate and in their own area of special interest.

Almost one-half of our kids grow up with interactive and immersive educational models where they can experience learning. Our kids take for granted multimedia as one of the ways we take in new information. We expect these kids to come to church on Sunday and learn about Jesus on . . . flanelgraph and blackboards. It has already been demonstrated that a mix of videos, readings, interactions with CD-ROMs or Web sites, and e-mail chat groups are far more important to today's learning than lectures.

It is difficult to get a man to understand something when his salary depends on not understanding it.

Upton Sinclair

In short, the changes in our learning paradigm require new structures and new core tools for the learning gene—active learning, interactive learning, mutual learning, team learning, service learning, game learning, leisure/vacation learning, adventure learning, electronic learning, network learning, group learning, distance learning, and cyberlearning systems and programs. Learning consultant Lewis J. Perelman has coined the term *"kanbrain"* (from the Japanese for "just-in-time delivery") to distinguish the drastic difference between learning and institutionalized education and training. "Kanbrain" learning incorporates new technologies such as knowledge-based systems, performance support, groupware, intranet that are designed to create, move, and apply knowledge, not deliver "instruction" or offer "courses."[10]

It took forty years to get the overhead projector out of the bowling alley and into the classroom. It must take less than that to get the computer into our ministries. Students who come from homes where the computer is commonplace (as of 1995, 40 percent of families had a home computer) already expect an IT component to enhance their instructional activities and learning opportunities.

If electronic forms of communication were to replace book-dominated education techniques as the basis of a new system of learning in the church, what would it look like?

First, verbal communication would be less important than communication through music, images, and art. In postmodern culture learning takes place more through arts than sciences.

Second, postmodern learning is personalized, digitized, globalized. The dominant means of learning and communication in the future will be the Web.

Third, churches would build new kinds of lecture halls or learning space: that is, television monitors and projectors suspended from the walls; computer-generated images and surround sound; a technician's assistance at all times; an "electronic blackboard" system that copies what is written on the blackboard directly into class members' laptop computers; video recording kept in the church library; live presentations sent over the network, allowing staff working in nurseries, and so forth. the option of watching from their ministry zones; and studio classrooms where the class can dissolve into small groups and work around stations that are hooked up to other stations, and then come back together.

III

The following paradigm shifts in educational expectations necessitate that we transcend the constraints of default but not defunct nineteenth-century hierarchy-bureaucracy styles of classroom learning, lecture learning, conference learning, and so forth.

The first shift: Where education was once thought of as a period of preparation for a lifetime of work, it is now seen as a lifetime of preparation for various work assignments. Perhaps the most important law of ecology is this: L≥C. It means that to survive, an organism's rate of learning must be equal to or greater than the rate of change in the environment. That is why the "learning organization" metaphor must be as applicable to church life as it is to corporate life.

We are all temps.
David M. Noer of the Center
for Creative Leadership

In the produce section of a large supermarket was posted this sign: "If you wish something that you don't see displayed, ask our perishable manager." Everything is perishable, especially information. Intellectual capital steadily depreciates unless it is refreshed and recycled. Vocational training is being replaced by the learning vocation—constant learning and unlearning or Life-Long-Learning.[11]

The more anyone is educated, the more education they seek. Baby boomers, the best-educated generation in history, are looking for life-long Elder hostel programs. The formalization of career continuing education means that learners expect to train continually for new vocational and volunteer opportunities. Nearly one third of all adults in the U.S. are currently enrolled in some kind of formal education program.[12] If formal continuing education is not available, self-education is a top priority.

The illiterate of the future are not those who cannot read or write, but those who cannot learn, unlearn and relearn.

Alvin Toffler

The second shift: Learning has been decentralized. Education is increasingly separated from the education system. The Wharton

School of Business at the University of Pennsylvania works with companies to design job-specific programs, which are then taught at Wharton. Some corporations are even applying for accreditation as institutions of higher education. If businesses are becoming institutions of higher education (corporate learning centers like General Motors and McDonald's, Motorola University and Disney University have ballooned from four hundred to one thousand in the last five years), why can't churches?

Actually, they are. For the first time the accrediting body of theological schools (ATS) granted accreditation in 1996 to a church as a full-fledged "seminary." Learners increasingly expect to learn in their homes and to receive academic credit for their efforts. Already distributed learning is a $7 billion market. The future belongs to those educational institutions that come to learners, and allow them to study and work at home as well as come to a campus for "intensives" and go on "retreats." Even places like Stanford and Harvard understand this. Stanford has embraced tele-education and is offering its courses via satellite across the U.S. Over thirty U.S. business schools (including both Stanford and Harvard) offer at least part of their MBA courses online. Duke's Fuqua School of Business boasts a Global Executive MBA Program where students converge electronically from all over the planet.

The third shift: Learners expect high quality education that connects them to global resources and multicultural learners. World knowledge doubles every four years. Half-lives of information are becoming smaller and smaller in every field. The half-life of most scientific knowledge (six years) and engineering knowledge (three years) is shrinking fast. Science-fiction writer Jerry Pournelle says that the computer industry is like a Third World country: there is a revolution every three months.

Cutting edges can quickly become dull edges. Unless leaders keep on their information toes, unless leaders work hard and diligently to stay hot and current, leaders automatically become obsolete by an information base for decision-making that gets more and more flawed, shaky, and eventually fatal. If ministers are not constantly learning and unlearning, they are becoming less and less qualified to serve as effective disciples of Jesus Christ. Postmodern leaders are constantly rebuilding themselves, embracing the young and opening themselves to the strange.

Scripture, reason, and experience jointly testify, that, inasmuch as the corruption of nature is earlier than our instructions can be, we should take all pains and care to counteract this corruption as early as possible. The bias of nature is set the wrong way: Education is designed to set it right. This, by the grace of God, is to turn the bias from self-will, pride, anger, revenge, and the love of the world, to resignation, lowliness, meekness, and the love of God.

John Wesley[13]

Peter M. Senge's 1990 classic *The Fifth Discipline* lays out the five core disciplines necessary to a "learning organization:"

1. **personal mastery**

2. **mental models**

3. **shared vision**

4. **team learning**

5. **systems thinking**[14]

A "smart" church or "learning organization"—one that embraces creativity, synergy, serendipity —will actually think creatively and adaptively as an organism, and will change itself without outside intervention. Failure to adapt and adjust to increasing complexity and accelerating change suggests a shutdown in one or more of the above-five disciplines: members may be too dependent; the vision may be unclear; there may be poor communication, or too few leaders; the team may not be functioning, or may be operating at only one level.

The fourth shift: Learners will require highly interactive computer mediated instruction through the programming and use of video, sound, and images embedded directly into the courseware. Through the "Mind Extension University,"[15] students already can get degrees from the University of Maryland and George Washington University (you register with the school, buy books, take classes on

TV, and take proctored exams in various cities). The more learners sit at the feet of the world's greatest teachers through televideophony, the more parishioners will expect access to the greatest theological minds and spiritual teachers of their time.

Chase if you can, bust if you must, but at all times, learn.

The Storm Chaser's motto

IV

Health care futurist Leland Kaiser is working with a variety of public and private organizations to create hospitals without walls, and to get health care services out of the hospital and into the community where the patient takes more responsibility for her or his own health.

The same needs to be done with theological education. One old/new model of serious theological education the church needs to consider is the "seminary" model. Every four years at General Conference the church debates whether it actually needs thirteen seminaries. Couldn't it do with fewer?

My response is that the problem with our church is not that we have too many seminaries, but that we have too few. Indeed, I shall not rest content until there are 42,000 seminaries in The United Methodist Church—one for each congregation.

The word "seminary" means literally "seed bed." If each congregation were to think of itself as a "seminary," a "seed bed for faith," and the ordained minister self-consciously became a "Dean," a whole new approach to the theological education of baptized ministers would result. Every "church" (aka "seminary") would build a distinguished faculty, a graduated curriculum of study for spiritual development, a full syllabi of courses (both required and elective) stressing how to live a disciplined Christian life.

51

The seminary model of theological education purposes the unleashing and releasing of ministry leadership among the baptized, showing them how to live as Christians and how to help others live as disciples of Christ. The seminary model features practical courses for everyday problems as well as more theoretical courses. It would also educate believers in "spirituality" that is both conscious and unconscious. In the words of Princeton sociologist Richard K. Fenn, "I can think of no higher priority to be placed before theological education and the continued education of the ministry than training in the language of the unconscious," which Erich Fromm called "God's forgotten language."[16] Graduation exercises and diplomas would mark successful movement from one level of training to another. The pastor should always teach the basic, required course "Christianity 101" for new members.

The role of graduate theological education centers needs to be expanded to help churches train their baptized ministers to become "faculty" for church seminaries. Jesus spent more time training his disciples than he did teaching the crowds. Through global education or "distance education," people with similar interests from around the globe can join together in taking an interactive course from the world's greatest biblical scholars and theologians—while moving educationally at their own learning speed. The classroom is dissolving into a vast international network of information and visual stimulation.

Church people will enter the seminary church curriculum and faculty at different levels and with different needs. It will go from cradle to grave—an education that goes all the way down to the nursery, which had better not be simply a place to park infants, but a place to provide emotional, intellectual, and most importantly, spiritual stimulation to infants.[17] In order to certify people for various ministries or faculty status, seminaries accredited by the Association of Theological Schools would partner with these teaching churches to grant credit for life experience to those who are not just starting out in their training, and who would make valuable local church seminary faculty. More experienced and trained staff could conceivably be exempted from some of the more basic curriculum.

NetNotes

http://www.leonardsweet.com/netbooks/gateways/

This NetNotes contains links to Albert Einstein, Oxford University, Drew University, Sunday school, Upton Sinclair, Stanford University, McDonalds, General Motors and various learning URLs. The Interactive page allows you to calculate the Wesley Spiritual Universe Theory. Selected images include the Cokesbury Bell, Cokesbury College and other learning related images. Your answers and comments about the "Rock-the-Cradle Discussion Questions and Genogram Exercises" can be posted on the Gateways Forum under the Learning/UnLearning Listing. The resources listing includes all indexed notes from the chapter, plus you can post additional resources under the Gateways Forum Learning/UnLearning Listing.

Rock-the-Cradle Discussion Questions and Genogram Exercises

1. In 1995 the British publication *The Economist* did a feature article on what it called "the death of distance."[18] Can you see signs that distance is dead? While distance is dead, is it the case that location is more alive and important than ever before?

2. The '96 Olds 88s inaugurated the smart-car era. For an extra $2,000, you can purchase the GuideStar, a navigation system that, with the push of a button and the purr of a trunk-mounted hard drive, will lead you or will lead your car by means of a map database to any destination in the country. You will never need a paper map (broadcast) again. Your media analog gives you door-to-door pointcasting precision.

   NavTech, maker of GuideStar, guarantees its database to be over 97 percent accurate. But information quickly perishes. If addresses and street names change 10 percent a year— which is a conservative estimate—then after two years the driver only has an 80 percent chance of reaching his/her destination. In other words: every year 10 percent of the information is *wrong*.

3. In ancient cosmology static was good; change was bad, even evil. What would it mean for the church to befriend change? Isn't there a need for a balance of stability and change?

4. Does it jar you to think that Jesus himself changed in the course of his ministry? Do a Bible study of the three "conversions" of Jesus, as outlined by biblical scholar and archaeologist Charles R. Page II. Jesus' first "conversion" moved him from the Hasidic fundamentalism of his Nazarene background to the Hillel liberalism of the Pharisees (Matthew 12:1-14). His second "conversion" experience, precipitated by his encounter with a Gentile woman in the region of Tyre and Sidon, moved him from seeing his ministry totally in terms of the Jewish community to reaching out to the Gentiles (Matthew 15:21-28). His third "conversion" experience led him to break with the Pharisees (Matthew 23:37-39) because of their establishment preoccupations and lack of concern for the people, and led to his death.[19]

5. How well does your church use ESP—*empathy, space,* and *pressure*—in handling resistance to change?[20] Sometimes people need understanding and compassion; other times they need time to move through the grief process and transition; other times they need subtle and even overt pressure to change. Which one of these does your church need now?

6. The book *Managing Transitions,* by William Bridges argues for the distinction between change and transition.[21] Change is an event that alters reality—for example, my eyesight deteriorates. Transition is the necessary adjustment to the alterations—for example, I get glasses and have to adopt an entirely new lifestyle. How is your church handling change, and handling transitions differently? Do you agree with Bridges that there *is* a difference?

7. If no one in your group has participated in the Boston-based Elderhostel program, invite someone in to talk about this peer-based educational residential program for people aged sixty and older. How might your church integrate this model into its own ministry? In the fall of 1991, almost 300,000 part-time students aged fifty and older enrolled as undergraduate, graduate, and professional students across the country. According to the Department of Education, almost 50,000 were enrolled full-time. How is your church addressing this need, which will only increase in the future with more and more boomers moving into retirement?

8. What would it take for your church to Get Smart? What would it look like for a church to have the smarts?

9. I no longer teach. I organize learning. What's the difference?

54

NINE

The CELL Gene

"A Prayer for Persons Joined in Fellowship"
Help us to help each other, Lord,
Each other's cross to bear,
Let all their friendly aid afford,
And feel each other's care.

Help us to build each other up,
Our little stock improve,
Increase our Faith, confirm our Hope,
And perfect us in Love.

Charles Wesley[1]

The human body is composed of little blocks of protoplasm called cells. So is the body of Christ. For Wesley the body of Christ was "cell grown."

It is time for the church to give up congregational thinking for cellular thinking. Indeed, it is in our genes to show the larger church how to "cell out." Methodism began as a cell group movement. In fact, the Methodist movement began in small, face-to-face groups most often characteristic of nature-based cultures. The organic "rules" behind one of the greatest outpourings of the Spirit in the history of the church, the closest Wesley ever came to a "magic formula" for transforming society, are these:

It was agreed by us,

1. That we will meet together once a week to "confess our faults one to another, and pray for one another that we may be healed."

2. That the persons so meeting be divided into several "bands," or little companies, none of them consisting of fewer than five or more than ten persons.

3. That everyone in order speak as freely, plainly, and concisely as he can, the real state of his heart, with his several temptations and deliverances, since the last time of meeting.

4. That all the bands have a conference at eight every Wednesday evening, begun and ended with singing and prayer.

5. That any who desire to be admitted into this society be asked, What are your reasons for desiring this? Will you be entirely open, using no kind of reserve? Have you any objection to any of our orders? (which may then be read).

6. That when any new member is proposed everyone present speak clearly and freely whatever objection he has to him.

7. That those against whom no reasonable objection appears be, in order for their trial, formed into one or more distinct bands, and some person agreed on to assist them.

8. That after two months' trial, if no objection then appear, they be admitted into the society.

9. That every fourth Saturday be observed as a day of general intercession.

10. That on the Sunday sennight [seven-night] following be a general love-feast, from seven till ten in the evening.

11. That no particular member be allowed to act in anything contrary to any order of the society; and that if any persons, after being thrice admonished, do not conform thereto, they be not any longer esteemed as members.[2]

In the organizational chart of early Methodism, there is no local church "congregation" to be found. In the famous 1822 "wheel-within-the-wheel" chart that explained the genius of the itinerant system, which in Methodist minds mirrored the motion of the solar system, the innermost revolving circle is the weekly band, then weekly classes, then monthly circuits, then quarterly districts, then annual conferences, and the outermost revolution the quadrennial general conference. The congregation was totally left out.

Wesley defined his "societies" as companies of individuals who united "in order to pray together, to receive the word of exhortation, and to watch over one another in love, that they may help each other to work out their salvation."[3] The heart of the Wesleyan methodology of discipleship was the cell known as the "class meeting," in effect a house church. In these cells Christians learned to, in Wesley's words, "'bear one another's burdens,' and 'naturally' to 'care for each other.' As they had daily a more intimate acquaintance with, so they had a more endeared affection for each other. And 'speaking the truth in love, they grew up into him in all things which is the head, even Christ.'"[4] When Wesley stated that "The gospel of Christ knows of no religion but social; no holiness but social holiness,"[5] or again "Christianity is essentially a social religion, and that to turn it into a solitary religion is indeed to destroy it,"[6] he did not so much mean social gospel or social action but "Christian conferencing." Discipleship must take place in community: to turn this religion into a solitary one is to destroy it.

How ironic that Paul Yonggie Cho, pastor of the largest church in the world of our day, encountered the key to his ministry in reading John Wesley's "cell out" of the church of his day. It was the Wesleyan question that began each cell meeting—"How goes it with your soul"—that brought the Yoido Full Gospel Church in Seoul, Korea, to almost three quarters of a million participants in 1995. Cho has proven Baptist missionary Ralph Neighbour correct in his contention that cells move church growth from addition to multiplication.[7] How ironic that a Korean Pentecostal and a Baptist missionary are better students of John Wesley than most Wesleyans.[8]

Unless the church travails, the soul is not born.
old Mennonite saying

What is a cell? A cell connects the spaces between people and the space within people. In a world that separates people from without and fragments them from within, connections are at the core of a healthy spirituality. Less abstractly, a cell is an intentional group of three to twelve people who gather together on a weekly basis for worship, outreach, discipleship, Bible study (often following the pastor's Sunday sermon), prayer, pastoral care, and evangelism. The cells do all of the seven pillars of the church of Acts: studying the Word, worship, prayer, evangelism, edification, care, and mission. Never larger than fifteen, they are to meet all the needs of the members as well as to disciple believers. Most especially, they are designed to train ministers and prepare leaders for ministry, and to teach the lesson of connectedness.

Members of home cells are taught to see themselves as ministers above all. Ralph Neighbour argues that the cells are to go through rituals of icebreakers, worship, edification, and vision sharing. Children remain with the adults during part of the cell, with special learning time with the children led by the adults at later times.[9] The cell group structure disciples believers, explores and exercises their spiritual gifts, provides primary caregiving to those hurting and broken, and keeps the community's focus upon evangelism and justice. In cells discipleship training enables believers to discover the freedom of conformity—being "conformed" to the likeness of Christ.

Home cell ministry moves each week from house to house (never more than two weeks in the same home), with constant dividing and subdividing every six months to a year. In the early church the needs of Christians were addressed in the homes, not the temple. The house church of Lydia (Acts 16:40), the house church of Nympha (Colossians 4:15), the house church at the home of Priscilla and Aquila (Romans 16:3-5), the house church of Philemon (Philemon 2) point out the obvious: "the New Testament church was in no sense a building" and "the house church was the common structural expression of the Christian congregation."[10] In fact, the early church did not construct church buildings until about A.D. 200.

Wherever something is wrong, something is too big.
**Austrian political philosopher
Leopold Kohr**[11]

The Methodist movement was started by someone who didn't want to go to church. The historical record reads that Wesley went "very unwillingly to a meeting in Aldersgate Street."[12] Our church began because someone who didn't want to go to church, went anyway. But the church John Wesley went to "very unwillingly" wasn't a church facility—it was a home. No more than thirty could have been at the Aldersgate Street meeting that night when Wesley's heart was strangely warmed.

Early Methodism, like the early church, went on in homes. The key, or basic unit, was not the congregation but the cell, called the "class," which was conducted in homes. Methodism was not centered in buildings, or congregations, or headquartered in some space. Rather, it was decentered in a variety of gatherings, events, and missions—bands (weekly), classes (weekly), circuits (monthly), districts [often same as camp-meetings] (quarterly), conferences (annual and quadrennial). It was in the homes that rituals like baptism, marriage, and the funeral took place. The organizational genius of Francis Asbury, Jacob Albright, Philip William Otterbein, and Phoebe Palmer was to build a spiritual movement around opposites—the small and the big, the simple and the complex: the class meeting and the camp-meeting, the broad "conferences" and the intimate "bands," the home cells and the outdoor revivals.

In fact, the religious rituals of Methodist laypeople revolved around the home. This changed, first in the early nineteenth century, when an "active church life" was patterned after the home but held in church facilities.[13] Second, it changed in the latter quarter of the nineteenth century, when "connectional" went from being people and gatherings following St. Paul's "Gifts of the Spirit" to bureaucratic programs and structures (local church, district offices, conference staff and agencies, later jurisdictional staff and programs, and national boards and agencies) following St. *Robert's Rules of Order.* The change was symbolized in 1872, when class leaders' and stewards' meetings changed into the "Official Board."

In the words of historian Russell Richey, "Methodist life was too dynamic, lay-centered and cooperative to be cooped up within congregations. Missional, flexible, adaptive, expansive, pluraform, decentralized, Methodism conducted its mission there, its education yonder, its baptisms and funerals here, its preaching over there, and so forth."[14]

59

The celling out of the Christian church is especially crucial in a world that has "demassified" to a "niche-or-be-niched" degree (Chuck Fromm) of market fragmentation. In typical both/and post-modern fashion, the more global the world we live in, the more individualized and customized any appeal must be. The extent to which micro-marketing has replaced mass marketing can be seen in everything from sneakers to spectacles. Before the Civil War shoe manufacturers didn't even niche the right and left feet. From one or two varieties of sneakers when I was growing up, there are now specialty sneakers for every sport conceivable. Bicycling shoes, for example, are even niched into off-road bicycling shoes, road bicycling shoes, and track bicycling shoes.

When is the last time you went to get some new eyeglasses? How many frame styles do you have to choose from? Sunglasses alone run into the hundreds—from one manufacturer. Or look how many narrow niche channels are now on TV? There is even a stamp collector's channel. There is no more GM (General Motors). There is only a variety of niche motors, a couple of which are niched to have more "mass" appeal. There are no more GPs (general practitioners). There are only a variety of specializations in medicine, one of which is niched as Family Medicine.

We are living in a world where there is no longer any "generally speaking." Doug Murren argues powerfully that niching "is even more vital to churches than it is to businesses."[15] One Bible distributor alone boasts that it carries an array of more than three thousand niche Bibles.[16] Unfortunately, the numbers of one-size-fits-all, one-service churches that are still out there prove that Henry Ford's "any-color-as-long-as-its-black" approach to people is still with us.

Niche evangelism is in the Wesleyan tradition's genes. The Wesleyan tradition has niche evangelism in its genes. One can see this in one of the most interesting letters Francis Asbury ever wrote, a letter that is in the archives of Barratt's Chapel. The letter was written to Ezekiel Cooper (1763–1847), a Freeborn Garretson convert who was conscripted into the itinerant ranks at this Barratt's Chapel service. Before everyone departed, Asbury asked the preachers present "if they knew of any young speaker in the circuit that would travel?" One of them recommended Cooper, and Cooper said yes.

In this letter from Asbury to Cooper, which was dated 23 December 1802, the Prophet of the Long Road complimented Cooper on his publishing efforts (Cooper took over from founder John Dickins [sic] the publishing enterprises that were later to become the Methodist Publishing House, the first denominational publishing house in America for books and church school literature). But Asbury suggested that Cooper needed to print his material in better binding for other evangelicals out here like Presbyterians. The cheap binding was sufficient for Methodists. But Presbyterians and Episcopalians wanted and needed better binding, and we should give it to them.[17]

No area exhibits the niche-gene more graphically than in the Methodist publication of hymnbooks. Cooper fell in love with "the small pocket hymnbook" which was first published in 1780 by a York, England, Methodist bookseller named Robert Spence. Spence pirated some Wesley hymns from a massive, 504-page collection called *Collection of Hymns for the Use of the People Called Methodists* and published it in a user-friendly form that could slip into one's pocket. Annoyed at being pirated and one-upped, Wesley published his own *Pocket hymnbook for the Use of Christians of All Denominations* in 1785.

Notice some things about these hymnbooks. See how healthy they look—dog-eared, battered, stained? Before the 1870s, hymnbooks were less parts of public worship than tools of the devotional life. They weren't kept in church for use in worship, but kept on one's person or by one's bedside for constant devotional use. The technology of pew racks, a Victorian invention, ended hymnbooks as a daily devotional resource for discipleship.[18] Early Methodists paved the road to Zion with their songs. When Wesley was in Walsingham, he began a service by standing in the streets of Walsingham and singing until people gathered. Then he preached.[19]

Methodist theology was conceived and conveyed less through texts and treatises than through songs, sermons and testimonies; less through propositions than through poetry and prayers. Music, and the melodies of our faith, are a part and parcel of our very being. Music is the heartbeat of the soul. Today the hymns we sing, and more precisely the way we sing, may actually be a part of our due punishment for sins.

We cannot live only for ourselves. A thousand fibers connect us with our fellow men; and among those

> *fibers, as sympathetic threads, our actions run as causes, and they come back to us as effects.*
>
> Herman Melville

Notice also that the hymnbooks laid out here are all of different sizes. There was no "one-size-fits-all" assumption. Hymns were published for every conceivable "niche"—children, youth, pockets, purses, camp-meetings, class-meetings, with music and without, for choir, quartet, solo, or mass singing. There were even what Kenneth Rowe calls "upstairs" and "downstairs" hymnals—the former for formal church services, the latter informal, folksy, sing-along services and Sunday school sessions. One of my favorites is the 1864 Sunday school hymnbook called *The Angel's Song*. If singing itself is an act of liberation, as W. H. Auden claimed ("Every high C accurately struck demolished the theory that we are the irresponsible puppets of fate or chance"), Methodists sought to set free every niche they could find through their hymnbooks.

Within a month after Asbury came to this country as a twenty-six-year-old preacher (1771), he resolved to get Methodism out of its urban fixation: "My brethren seem unwilling to leave the cities, but I think I shall show them the way . . . for I am determined to make a stand against all partiality."[20] Wesley trained his preachers to reach out toward all social groups. The character of a Methodist, Wesley argued, is to "do good unto all":

> . . . unto neighbours, and strangers, friends, and enemies. And that in every possible kind; not only to their bodies, by "feeding the hungry, clothing the naked, visiting those that are sick or in prison," but much more does he labour to do good to their souls, as of the ability which God giveth: to awaken those that sleep in death; to bring those who are awakened to the atoning blood, that "being justified by FAITH" they may have peace with God; and to provoke those who have peace with God to abound more in love and in good works. And he is willing to "spend and to be spent herein," even to "be offered upon the sacrifice and service of their faith," so they may "all come unto the measure of the stature of the fullness of Christ."[21]

The stretch was personally painful to him, an Oxford don and one of the most eminent scholars of his day (onetime fellow of

Lincoln College). The truth is Wesley resisted field preaching until George Whitefield finally ground him down and Wesley said he'd give it a try: "Having been all my life . . . so tenacious on every point relating to decency and order that I should have thought the saving of souls *almost a sin* if it had not been done *in a church.*"[22] What changed Wesley's mind? One Sunday afternoon in 1739, as Whitefield and Wesley approached a hill outside Bristol, he saw over three thousand people standing and waiting for spiritual food. The sight moved him to change: "I submitted to be more vile, and began to preach . . . and proclaimed the glad tidings."[23]

At that moment Wesley resolved to reach the unchurched masses—and to do so he went to the mines, factories, prisons, streets, and fields. Like few others in the history of the Christian church, Wesley delivered the goods of the gospel for the masses. One minute Wesley was capable of speaking to Oxford scholars. The next moment he communicated through "street stories" to the working classes in their homes, to farmers in their fields, to laborers in their factories, to prisoners in their cells, to miners in their pits, to weavers at their looms.

When John Wesley finished writing a sermon, he wasn't finished. He would then read it to his maid and eliminate any words she didn't understand. One of the greatest minds of the Enlightenment Era and Industrial Age learned how to reach the six-pack culture of his day.

What informational fields and factories is Christ calling us to enter? How "vile" are we the descendants of Wesley willing to be for the gospel? One out of five Americans is illiterate. Another one out of five Americans reads at a third-grade level. How vile will your church get to reach adult minds with children's literacy? Zondervan's "New International Reader's Version" bills itself as the "first-ever Bible written at a 2.9 grade reading level."[24] Houston educator P. K. McCary has written a version of the New Testament for African-American teenagers called "Rappin' With Jesus: The Good News According to the Four Brothers."[25]

How "vile" will you become to reach for Christ another generation other than your own? How willing are you to support "vile" ministries that go beyond the boosters (No Sweat), ministries to boomers (No Problem), busters (No Fear) and millennial kids (No Worries) that will cause you to raise your traditional eyebrows?

For the church to "cell out," to be sure, does not mean for it to "sell out." The human body boasts two kinds of cells: somatic cells, which constitute most of the body, and gametic cells (or germ line cells), which are sex-reproductive cells found in the ova and sperm. When somates are altered, the changes die with the body. Once gametes are altered, however, the changes are unalterable and get passed on to succeeding generations. The niching of ministry for a variety of constituencies must never tamper with the gamete cells of the Christian faith, only the somate cells. Somates must change, or die. The vocabulary of the "meta-church" is based on the word "meta," which means change.

Or to state this point using Jesus' own image for the gospel, "living waters" will fill any space or container without changing its content. To "cell out" is to get people to pick up the *content* that they might "taste-and-see" how good the "living water" actually is using whatever *container* works. To "sell out" is to add to, subtract from, or mess with the *content* as well as the *container*.[26]

NetNotes
http://www.leonardsweet.com/netbooks /gateways/

The Cell Gene NetNotes has links to Henry Ford, Mennonites, Wesley Discipleship Program, Cokesbury, Maxwell House, Yoido Full Gospel Church in Seoul and various cell related URLs. Selected images include the Asbury & Cooper Letter, an assortment of hymnbooks and other cell related images. Your answers and comments about the "Rock-the-Cradle Discussion Questions and Genogram Exercises" can be posted on the Gateways Forum under the Cell Listing. The resources listing includes all indexed notes from the chapter, plus you can post additional resources under the Gateways Forum Cell Listing.

Rock-the-Cradle Discussion Questions and Genogram Exercises

1. The Bible, argues Neal F. McBride, portrays Jesus Christ "as the greatest small group leader in history."[27] Would you agree?
2. According to historian Russell Richey, the basic question is where is Methodism most "at home"?

   Will it be at home only in its buildings, under corporate management, controlled by pastors, programmed only from one center, hemmed in by local bureaucratic procedure, preoccupied with accountability? Or will Methodism re-enter the homes of its people, and more importantly, the people who need to hear its message? Will it move out of its buildings into its neighborhoods? Will it become again too dynamic, lay-centered and cooperative to be cooped up within a congregation? Will it reclaim its missional, flexible, adaptive, expansive, pluraform, de-centralized ecclesial principle?[28]

   How would you answer Richey's question?
3. Take your group to the neighborhood coffee bar. How many different kinds of specialty coffees are being offered? Count how many different ways you can order what used to be a simple exchange of

   "Coffee, please."

   "Cream or sugar?"

   My coffee order is "Tall latte double skinny, please." (That means a double shot of espresso served in latte [not cappuchino] fashion made with skimmed milk.) One day I had said too many times "Tall latte double skinny, please" but found myself unable to resist a Starbucks. So I went in and asked for a "Tall latte double skinny sleeper, please." The attendant smiled and barked at her colleague at the espresso machine, "This guy wants a 'Why bother.'"

   Maxwell House, Folger's, Nescafe and other mass brands that used cheap beans to make similar-tasting coffee are in trouble. These three brands, with a 90 percent share of the market as recently as 1987, have been trounced by gourmet roasters that have created more than one billion dollars in shareholder value. People want better-tasting, gourmet, flavored, specialty coffees. To order general coffee, you now have to ask for it: "Regular coffee, please."

In a world that demands quality, even in its coffee (hence the Starbucks phenomenon), on any Sunday morning, in any community across this nation, where is the *worst* coffee in town served?

What are the implications of "niche-or-be-niched" for your church?

4. Someone once said that "temperamental musicians" were half temper and half mental. Should music ministers be dedicated to helping you to experience and glorify God? Or should they be devoted to teaching you to sing and appreciate "good music"?

5. According to the *Oxford English Dictionary*, "vile" can describe a morally depraved, despicable character. But in the eighteenth century it could also refer to any person considered worthless or of no account. When Wesley wrote of submitting himself to become more vile, it meant that he was stooping down to reach those persons for whom English society held no esteem or regard. Today, we might describe it as doing something tacky, uncouth, or in bad taste. How has your church reached down to minister? What tacky, grubby, or uncouth things have you done lately?

6. Get a copy of the two translations mentioned above: *Rappin' with Jesus* and *New International Readers Version*, or any other versions you are interested in, and compare the birth narratives in Matthew's Gospel.

7. Discuss the proposed five phases in the life cycle of a small group or cell, according to Neal F. McBride in his important practical handbook on *How to Build Small Groups Ministry* .

   1) Forming—birth and infancy (2–3 sessions)
   2) Norming—childhood (6–7 sessions)
   3) Conforming—adolescent (5–6 sessions)
   4) Performing—maturity (30 sessions)
   5) Reforming—old age and demise (5–6 sessions)
   6) back to (1)

   Use this hands-on handbook to build a cell ministry in your church.

8. There are numerous variations in home cell groups: home Bible studies, home fellowship groups, home cell groups, base-satellite units (missional house churches sponsored by a host church, usually meeting on Sunday morning in homes), house churches,

and so forth. Which kinds do you already have in your church? Are there already "cells" meeting in your church building?

9. The magazine for the global cell church movement is called *CellChurch Magazine.*[29] Each issue includes some sample "ice-breakers" (e.g., "Where do you go or what do you do when life gets too stressful for you? Why?" or "When you were a child, what did you want to be when you grew up? What did your parents want you to be?" or "What is one quality that you value or admire in one or more members of this group?" or "Does your name have a special meaning and/or were you named after someone special?" or "If you could ask Christ to change one problem in the world today, what would you like Him to change?").

It also includes a sample "cell church" meeting agenda. Here is one from page 12 of the winter 1996 issue:

Icebreaker (10 Minutes)

Share with us something unique about your wedding, a wedding you went to, or a wedding you participated in.

Praise and Worship (25 Minutes) UP-REACH

Ask one person to read Psalm 108:1-6; if children are present in your group, ask them to read it in unison together for the adults. Then, if you know it, sing the praise song taken from this passage: "Be exalted, O God, above the heavens and Thy glory above all the earth." Share in a season of praise prayers, using short sentences and enjoying being in God's presence.

Topic for Discussion

TOPIC: Matthew 25:1-13 (Go around the circle and have each person read a verse starting with Matthew 25:1 until you reach Matthew 25:13. Ask these questions for discussion.

1. Who is the bridegroom?
2. Who are the ten virgins?
3. What does the oil represent?
4. In what ways can we be ready for the Second Coming?

Ministry (35 Minutes) IN-REACH

If there are some non-Christians in your group: At the final wedding banquet, where will you be standing and why?

If there are only Christians: In what ways do you need more of His Spirit?

Prayer Time

Split into groups of two or three. Have group members pray over each other according to what was just discussed. Come back into the big group. Pray especially for the needs of new people in the group. Pray a prayer of blessing on their lives.

Share the Vision: (10 Minutes) OUT-REACH

The only way really to be prepared is to receive the Life of Jesus Christ . . . believing on Him intellectually, but surrendering your whole being as a vessel to be filled with His Holy Spirit. Each week we meet to encourage, pray, and minister to one another. As we learn to love and trust one another and grow in our walk with Jesus, we want to add new members so they too can experience the intimacy we have found.

EIGHT

The STACKING Gene

*It's not an assembly line. . . . I don't write first, then
design, then shoot. I'm doing everything together.*
Star Wars creator/
digital emperor George Lucas[1]

When *Moby-Dick* (1851) first came out, it flopped. So badly did it flop, in fact, that Herman Melville sank into a deep depression, and was prescribed a trip to the Mediterranean in hope of a cure. After a couple more commercial disasters, Melville took the job of customs inspector, which supported his family from 1866 to 1885. He died in 1891, in almost total obscurity, and wasn't rediscovered until about 1920.

Why was the culture of Melville's day unable to appreciate his genius? The strength of *Moby-Dick* today was its weakness in the nineteenth century: its multiple meanings, its plural dimensions, its distributed selves, its stacking abilities.

A scale-model of the earliest Barratt's Chapel reveals something about our roots that we have forgotten. Flaps girdle the inside of the church. Both downstairs and in the balcony there are flaps that can be lowered and raised to create different space usages.

In other words, the original Barratt's Chapel was a multiple use facility. A class meeting and a worship service could be going on at the same time. The flaps that went up and down in both the balcony and the main floor allowed for a variety of things going on at the same time or in the same space.

The Wesleyan movement in the U.S. began with the "Stacking Gene."

I

My favorite "Gumpism" has nothing to do with chocolates, but everything to do with "stacking." The thread that ties the movie classic *Forrest Gump* together is Gump's jogging. The "Gumpism" associated with his running is this: "When the body is most in motion, the mind is most at rest."

I call this principle "stacking." Other observers are calling the stacking gene by other names. Mary Parker Follett calls it "multiple leadership" (simultaneous functioning in the roles of leader, follower, and peer). Charles Handy calls it Portfolio Living (he wants us to "think portfolio"). Darryl Hartley-Leonard, president of Hyatt Hotels, calls this "silo-busting" (Hyatt crosstrains employees in multiple tasks to provide better service and save money).

Being a Genius is being one who is at one and the same time telling and listening to anything and everything.

Gertrude Stein[2]

Stacking was first taught to me by my West Virginia gramma, Ida Boggs (one of whose favorite expressions was "You can kill two birds with one stone"), who would hold me on her lap (that's one thing) and tell me stories (that's doing two things at once) while she knitted (that's three) all the while she was rocking (that's four and five—one has to work to relax in a rocker).

I next learned stacking when an elementary school gym teacher tried to teach my class (my Baptist feet watched from the sidelines) to do the Brazilian dance called the "samba." The art of samba is the trick of stacking. Samba requires the upper body to be still while the lower body from the waist down gyrates and writhes like crazy.

70

I learned stacking in high school when our church organist eloped one Saturday, and our pastor (the Rev. Walter J. Whitney) called me out of a piano lesson to see if I wouldn't step into the breach and play an instrument I had never touched—a pipe organ with three keyboards for the hands and one for the feet.

I watch stacking every time I turn on "The Late Show with David Letterman" and see how Paul Shaffer plays several synthesizers at once.

Modern man no longer works at what cannot be abbreviated.

Paul Valery

There is a classic photograph illustrating what I mean by stacking. It appeared in the *Naples Daily News* (14 July 1996) and shows Michael Feldman taking a Saturday morning jog near his home in North Naples. Staff photographer Hope Kinchen caught him exercising on skates, listening to a walkman, clocking his mileage with wrist odometers, all while pushing his year-old daughter Mia in a jogging stroller while she is holding on to a Barney balloon.

It's not true that you can't be in two places at once—that's what virtual reality is all about. It's not true that you can only do one thing at a time. The real truth is "You can never only do one thing."[3] Forrest Gump was even doing two things that were opposite at the same time: his body was sweating and wearing down, and his mind was being renewed and gearing up. Or in the promise of Scripture, our bodies can be decaying, while our souls get better and more Godlike (2 Corinthians 4:7-12). Life is multidimensional. All of us live in multi-storied structures. While we can *be* on any one floor at a time, we live on and out of different levels.

On a quantum level, we are both particle and wave: we have particle states, and we have nonlocal wave states. The quantum mechanical wavefunction of a system can embody two or more mutually exclusive configurations at the same time. Physicist/Trekkie Lawrence M. Krauss illustrates this stacking phenomenon (or as

71

physicists like to call it, the "many worlds phenomenon") that is at the heart of the quantum universe:

> For example, if a particle is spinning clockwise, we say that its spin is "up." If it is spinning counterclockwise, we say that its spin is "down." Now, the quantum mechanical wavefunction of this particle can incorporate a sum with equal probabilities: spin up and spin down. If you measure the direction of the spin, you will measure *either* spin up *or* spin down.[4]

The quantum world of simultaneity, of all-at-onceness, can be illustrated by our five senses—hearing, seeing, tasting, touching, smelling—which work together to integrate different simultaneous stimuli into one stacked sensation. The brain functions by means of what cognitive psychologists call "parallel distributed processing" (PDP), a passing of patterns "through a large configuration of synaptic connections." This is very different from the "serial processing" found in conventional computers, which process in logical, linear, one-at-a-time predetermined sequences ("programs").

Readers beware! There are more selves to your self than meets the eye!

University of Chicago
scholar Sander Gilman

Stacking is second nature to most members of the postmodern generation. Kids today have strong parallel processing skills. Look at their video games, where everything happens at once, where one has to deal with everything at the same time. No wonder their abilities at linear, sequential, serial thought are less than their forebears. Skilled at computer graphics by age five, they go to church and get . . . flannelgraphs. Computer experts by age six, they go to school and get . . . blackboards. Unable to sit there non-interactively and concentrate while we lecture them for hours on end, we diagnose them as having Attention Deficit Disorder (ADD)—and put them on class-two controlled substances called amphetamines so they will sit there and focus on our outmoded educational methods.

Radio is the ultimate stacking technology—you can drive, exercise, work, clean, or read while listening. Is that why there has been a huge growth in the radio listening public? "One of the dominant trends in media use over the last 30 years is an increased tendency to watch or listen to a program while doing something else. 'Secondary activity,' in the Americans' Use of Time Project, is defined as something done in conjunction with some other primary activity. About one-fourth of the time Americans spend with television is secondary activity. More than 90 percent of their time with radio is secondary."[5] USAmericans spend more than ten hours a week of radio listening while doing something else.

II

There was an old saying about the Methodists: While other parsons were crossing the t's on their Sunday sermon manuscripts, the Methodist preacher had evangelized and set up three congregations. Our forebears were able to do so much so quickly because they thought in multiples. Successful in creating multiple alternative forms of popular entertainment, they even persuaded the sponsors of the suspect entertainment to follow the guidelines of an evangelical Protestant moral system.[6]

From day one Methodists exhibited a multi-mindedness that was characteristic of apostolic times. Multiple worship services are not new. Multi-service worship was the model of the New Testament. The early church was a multi-service church. It was built on a multi-service model. Apostolic Christians met every day in homes in small groups, and they met weekly in large groups for temple court celebrations.[7]

The restoration of apostolic Christianity was the peculiar mission of Methodism.[8] Francis Asbury believed that the apostolic order, which was lost in the first century and only partly restored by the Reformation, was fully reintroduced in America. "In 1784, an apostolic form of Church government was formed in the United States of America at the first General Conference of the Methodist Episcopal Church held at Baltimore, in the State of Maryland." It was the function of Methodism to "restore and retain primitive order; we

73

must, we will, have the same doctrine, the same spirituality, the same power in ordinances, in ordination, and in spirit."[9]

Part of the apostolic spirit was manifested in the appointment of "itinerants" to a circuit with multiple "charges," where each charge was unique and different. In the multicongregational model of early Methodism, each worship experience became a different congregation. The pastor remained the same. The congregations may have even met in different buildings. But they shared a common governance. It is an indication of how far United Methodists have departed from our genes when it is even a question of whether or not to have multiple worship services for different "charges" entrusted to our care.

The United Methodist Church is multicultural at its base—it has an Anglo side, and it has a German side, it has a fire side and it has an ice side, it has a white side and it has a black side, it has an Anglican side, and it has a Reformed side. To open the *Discipline* and to explore the doctrinal standards brought to the union of both the German side and the Anglo side is to see a church that is omni-dimensional at its core, a church that stacked itself from the very beginning.

Don't be afraid of having too many irons in the fire, if the fire is hot enough.

Anonymous

E. M. Forster used to distinguish between "flat people," who are one-dimensional, and "round people," who are multi-faceted. Postmoderns are "round people" par excellence. We already live well-rounded, well-stacked lives amid dizzyingly complex, multiple, and interlinked forces. We have stacked households—more than one income. We already have stacked careers—"re-careering" and "multi-careering" have replaced the outmoded concept of "career." We have stacked relationships—more than one friend. We stack caring for the family, managing a career, tending aging parents, pursuing meaningful activities in a "do-it-all" life. We even have stacked intelligences, or what Howard Gardner calls "multiple intelligences." Gardner has isolated seven different ways cognitive learning takes place in the brain from which each of us selects our preferred ways of learning.[10]

The answers to the following queries will show you what "the stacking experience" is all about.

- Why are the three best-selling vehicles in America today trucks (about 20 percent of the 1995 market), sport-utility vehicles (over 10 percent of the market in 1995, with more than twenty-five models and styles), and minivans (these family rooms on wheels comprise about 8.4 percent of the market in 1995)? Why are sport-utility vehicles the number one pick of women, the gender most responsible for purchasing vehicles?
- Why did Tums climb back to the top of its category when SmithKline Beecham started advertising Tums as not just an antacid but also as a calcium supplement?
- Why have Tiger Mart convenience stores hooked up with Exxon gas stations?
- Why did Mentadent toothpaste emerge almost overnight? Why are millions swishing the almost impossible to use Mentadent mouthwash?
- Why do Chubbs baby-wipes, made by Sterling Winthrop, Inc., come in one of four bright colors? The plastic boxes are interlockable, allowing babies to play with them and literally stack them, and parents to save them as containers.
- Why is there a perforation in the lid of the jars of Bug City, a candy tart made by Amurol Confections? So kids can use the jars to keep bugs in when the candy is gone.
- Why is a watch that does nothing but keep time an endangered species, doomed to antiquedom? Why is the Dick Tracy watch already here?[11] Why are watches being made now with multiple faces for people who live in multiple time zones?
- Why is "Sit & Spin" such a success on the West Coast? Because it functions as an urban cafe *and* laundromat *and* restaurant *and* . . .
- Why is Barnes & Noble the market leader in bookstores (which they have made into entertainment centers, cafes, and the like), with over 350 discount superstores and 625 smaller shops?

75

- Why are scientists this very minute experimenting with "wearable computing" or "softwear" with which you could send spoken messages through your lapel, or receive audio communications through an earring?[12]
- Why is *Waxweb* (an interactive film, an illustrated text, a Web site, and a MOO— all rolled into one) so hard to describe?

Postmodern culture is fascinated with multiples, from Eddie Murphy in *The Nutty Professor* to Michael Keaton in *Multiplicity* to Portuguese poet Fernando Pessoa, called the greatest European poet of the twentieth century, who before he drank and smoked eighty cigarettes a day) himself to death at forty-seven had created no less than sebenty-two heteronymns (other names for himself), three of which (Alberto Caeiro, Ricardo Reis and Alvaro de Campos) earned him his global acclaim. Multiple personality disorder, Sherry Turkle contends in *Life on the Screen*, is almost a "paradigmatic illness of our time, almost an epidemic, the way hysteria . . . was the paradigmatic illness of Freud's time."[13] Postmoderns mix and match, and flaunt mixed metaphors: we combine computer programming with rural farm living; we stack Jhane Barnes designs with Rush Limbaugh politics; we mix Kentucky Fried Chicken with diet Pepsi; we mix the theme music of lowbrow TV ("Wheel of Fortune") with The Three Tenors.

III

The stacking phenomenon, which splices together multiple perspectives, multiple paths, multiple styles, and multiple celebrities resulting in something greater and more beguiling than the sum of its parts, can be found everywhere in the business and educational worlds as well. Long-distance calling cards are used more often, it is found, if they offer other services like electronic messaging and stock quotations. Boston-area train commuters are earning college credits en route through Dean Junior College, which teaches on board the Massachusetts Bay Transit Authority Trains. New York City cabs are featuring pay phones in back seats. In a desire to "combine business and pleasure," there is an ever-increasing use of out-of-the-office settings for business discussions: golfing and business, drinks and business, high tea and business, dinner and business, to name but a few. Frequent flier miles have become a permanent feature of the airline industry because of this stacking phenomenon. In fact, to help pay for the program the airline industry now sells frequent flier miles at two cents apiece to just about anyone who wants them—furniture makers, mortgage lenders, charities, and restaurants. American Airlines alone made $300 million in 1995 selling miles to businesses.

Microsoft has bet much of its future on the power of stacking. There is only one reason to buy Windows 95—your desire to "multitask," to work on multiple things at the same time. The frequency of the future is wireless, as worldwide, one new telephone subscriber in six opts for a cellular phone. But the phones now being developed for the future feature portability and twenty-four-hour reachability through the stacking of services (such as satellite, cellular and PHS) which would switch automatically depending on the incoming call.

It has been said that channel surfing is the closest many of us come to a participatory sport. Literary editor of *The New Republic*, Leon Wieseltier, speaks for the whole complement of poly-attentive, channel-surfing generations who have no problem investing in multiple activities on-screen at the same time: "I hear it said of somebody that he is leading a double life. I think to myself—Just 2?"[14] You just don't have one identity. You have many identities. "You" is plural.

We must learn to be plural, as truth is plural. Isn't the doctrine of the Trinity precisely this: there can be three Persons but one Being? Every one of us is plural, not singular, while still one being. My mongrelhood is primarily Anglo-Welshness—a tangy broth of Welsh wildness and English mildness; Welsh loquaciousness and English taciturnity; Welsh poetry, English prose. Psychologist Alfred Schutz has shown how a person inhabits many worlds. This is demonstrated by historian Martin E. Marty in an illustration adapted for the postmodern temper:

> One can be a mother, a specialist in biblical studies, an insecure untenured person delivering a lecture, a spouse, a person who has just been told she has a malignant tumor, and an enjoyer of Scarlatti, and live in all the worlds these situations represent.

Marty posits further that this person is giving a lecture on the book of Ruth, and suddenly has a stab of pain in her neck tumor. Expressing in the former case and experiencing in the latter may make her momentarily unaware of the smiling spouse in the audience or the scowlingly enigmatic Committee on Tenure in the audience. She may look forward to the post-lecture recital, but cannot be thinking about it now, even though she has rehearsed to take her turn in the ensemble.[15]

This fanciful postmodern human does not stack contradictory roles. In Marty's closing words about this phenomenon, "On stage, which is what all life is, we may be one persona but we carry the penumbra of others, without contradiction or conflict."[16]

What is necessary is that we learn to move more freely, more adventurously, in the stories of God.
Gerard Loughlin[17]

You and I are many stories, we are many selves, we are multiple identities. The doctrine of the Trinity is that God is three stories in one story. Part of postmodern leadership is helping people to do more than drift in and out of various roles. William James did not go far enough when he talked about our living a "two-storied" life. We all live out of multiple stories. We must learn how to navigate with integrity through multiple roles and stories. "Gary" from Reading, Pennsylvania, is a real person. He's a hairstylist. But while he has a captive audience sitting in that chair, he also sells hot tubs . . . and water coolers . . . and water purifiers . . . and legal services . . . and rents apartments. Here's someone who can coach the rest of us in "stacking."

In the words of the chief anthropologist of cyberspace, Sherry Turkle, "The goal of healthy personality development is not to become a One, not to become a unitary core, it's to have a flexible ability to negotiate the many—cycle through multiple identities." Rather than build a unitary self, a One personality, Turkle suggests we must learn how to "cycle through" many personalities.[18]

I would argue we must be both single and multiple, but the singularity comes as an integration of the multiples. Rather than the "One" being the result of multiples "fitting in," the One is the result of multiples "fitting together."

Postmodern Christians must live in multiple worlds—the ancient world (the world of the Bible and church history), the world in which we grew up, and the contemporary world (the postmodern world in which we live). In fact, if you can't live in both worlds at once, you can't do ministry in the twenty-first century. Why? Because the postmodern church—with its decentralized, movement-oriented, relational, nonclerical focus—is more first century than anything else.

Postmodern churches must live in multiple generational cultures simultaneously—boosters, boomers, busters, and the millennial kids. Postmodern churches must live in multiple ethnic cultures simultaneously—Asian, African, Latino, and so on.

IV

But beware: the laws of physics say that while you inhabit many worlds at the same time, you can never experience more than one world at a time. In other words, one can only be present to one world at a time.

Even a practiced juggler can only keep so many balls in the air at once. There are no limitations, but there are limits. We live in a world of limitless horizons. But "the sky's the limit." While we learn no limitations, we must learn our own speed limits. Every one of us travels at different speeds. Every one of us must learn our biological speed limits, our psychological speed limits, our intellectual speed limits, even our devotional speeds. Each one of us is different.

Take the last, our devotional prayer life, as an example. A woman wrote Wesley that she was dry spiritually. She professed to be rising at dawn to do her devotions. She confessed to daily reading her Bible and weekly attendance at church. She was doing all the right things, but her faith was growing cold. What should she do?

Wesley wrote back matter-of-factly, even curtly. You may need to rise before dawn. You may need to read your Bible multiple times a day. You may need to attend church often during the week. Some of us need to work harder at these things than others.

In order to move to the particular, in order to focus creativity, in order to bring definition to limitless existence, one must embrace limits. I am writing this book because I choose not to do some other things. I may be writing many books at the same time, but I can only write one book at once. When I said "yes" to this book, I said "no" to some other books.

If I had known what it would be like to have it all, I might have settled for less.

Lily Tomlin

In any given moment, you and I cannot "have it all." In spite of what Lily Tomlin says, no one can "have it all." All we can have is that for which we are willing to sacrifice, value most, and pay the cost.

Freedom is not the absence of limits, or pursuing infinite possibilities or infinite stackings. True freedom is choosing and acquiescing in limits, and connecting oneself to real possibilities. Where our potential meets the possibilities the world has to offer is where we must live. The composer Igor Stravinsky said it best:

> I have the seven notes of the scale and its chromatic intervals at my disposal . . . strong and weak accents are within my reach, and . . . in all these I possess solid and concrete elements which offer me a field of experience just as vast as the upsetting and dizzy infinitude that had just frightened me. . . . What delivers me from the anguish into which an unrestricted freedom plunges me is the fact that I am always able to turn immediately to the concrete things that are here in questions. . . . Whatever diminishes constraint diminishes strength."[19]

Complete freedom is the end of freedom. The Spirit makes us more free by helping us work within limits as finite, contingent creatures.

NetNotes
http://www.leonardsweet.com/netbooks /gateways/

Included with this NetNotes are links to Moby Dick, *Forrest Gump*, David Letterman, *The Nutty Professor* and various stacking related URLs. The Interactive page contains an animation of Barratt's chapel multi-purpose building where you watch stacking elements take place. Click a provided link to a Net Radio station, and experience stacking cyber style. Selected images include Barratt's Chapel and other stacking type images. Your answers and comments about the "Rock the Cradle Discussion Questions and Genogram Exercises" can be posted on the Gateways Forum under the Stacking Listing. The resources listing includes all indexed notes from the chapter, plus you can post additional resources under the Gateways Forum Stacking Listing.

Rock-the-Cradle Discussion Questions and Genogram Exercises

1. In the course of one week's normal watching of TV commercials, have your group identify how many commercials appeal to the stacking gene.
2. Have someone setup for demonstration Tennessee Dixon's CD-ROM *ScruTiny in the Great Round*.[20] See how many people ask: "What is it? Is it art? Is it entertainment? Is it musical compositions? Is it poetry? Is it meditation?" The answer, of course, is that it's all the above . . . and more. The box reads "Enter a magically interactive dreamscape through which you wander and make astonishing discoveries. Or just relax and savor the paintings, poetry, and music that ebb and flow at your command. Navigate through a banquet of interwoven images, metaphoric icons, audible symbols, and words. Most software titles merely allow you to open files and manipulate data. *ScruTiny in the Great Round* allows you to open your mind and manipulate your perspective."
3. Explore how your church can "stack" its ministry by researching which long-distance carriers will use some of your money to make a difference in our world.

81

For example, Working Assets Long Distance Network ("We Make Your Voice Heard": 800/INFO-735) is a phone company that supports environmental causes by donating 1 percent to non-profit groups working for peace, human rights, economic justice and the environment—donations that don't cost you a penny. In 1995 Working Assets gave two million dollars to groups like Greenpeace and Human Rights Watch. With each phone bill comes an update on key issues facing Washington, along with free phone calls to targeted decision makers around the world.

4. There is a contemporary Christian music group called "Jars of Clay" that have broken into the Top 40 secular market along with Amy Grant and Michael W. Smith. In 1996 they opened for Sting, and sold 700,000 copies of their debut album. Listen to their song "He," and see if you can't identify the musical stacking that is going on in this one song. Diverse musical instruments (some traditional, some ethnic) seem at times to be going off in their own directions. Yet amid the chaos there is order and melody and harmony.

5. Here is an exercise that explores the life-giving properties of limits. Ask the class to "draw anything." See how confused, blank, argumentative, and noncreative the rsponses are. Then ask the class to "draw anything as long as it is a _____." Now see how creative, inventive, and productive they can be.

6. Are there some jobs where "stacking" or "multitasking" is a prerequisite? How about Starbucks?

SEVEN

The TEAM Gene

I can't turn this series into some personal redemption. My redemption is to get back to where I was [a member of a champion team]. My redemption does not come from individuality.

His Airness Michael Jordan[1]

A mule named "Jim" was being driven by his owner. When everyone got on the wagon, the driver yelled "Giddyup Jim. Giddyup Sue. Giddyup Sam. Giddyup Sara. Giddyup Joe."

As the wagon started to move, one of the passengers said: "When Jim is the only one pulling, why did you call all those other names?"

The owner replied: "If Jim knew he was the only one pulling this wagon, he'd never budge an inch."

It takes teamwork to move anything, including birds. Something as simple as the geometrics of flocking starlings reveal the embeddedness of the team gene throughout creation itself. In 1987, computer scientist Craig Reynolds simulated on-screen the flocking abilities of wild birds, which he playfully termed "boids." In Reynolds's programming of the computer, not once did he intimate, much less direct, that the individual "boids" stay together or work as a team.

Reynolds's program simply directed a bunch of individual birds to fly around a screen full of walls and barriers. Each "boid" was programmed to follow three simple rules of behavior. M. Mitchell Waldrop, in his book *Complexity*, summarizes the three rules:

83

1. It tried to maintain a minimum distance from other objects in the environment, including other boids.
2. It tried to match velocities with boids in its neighborhood.
3. It tried to move toward the perceived center of mass of boids in its neighborhood.[2]

Waldrop says that teams form, not from the top down, but from the bottom up. Indeed, one doesn't even need to tell people to "form a flock" or "form a team" the team gene is so hardwired into our brains.

> What was striking about these rules was that none of them said, "Form a flock." Quite the opposite: the rules were entirely local, referring only to what an individual boid could see and do in its own vicinity. If a flock was going to form at all, it would have to do so from the bottom up, as an emergent phenomenon. And yet flocks *did* form, every time. Reynolds could start his simulation with boids scattered around the computer screen completely at random, and they would spontaneously collect themselves into a flock that could fly around obstacles in a very fluid and natural manner. Sometimes the flock would even break into subflocks that flowed around both sides of an obstacle, rejoining on the other side as if the boids had planned it all along. In one of the runs, in fact, a boid accidentally hit a pole, fluttered around for a moment as though stunned and lost, then darted forward to rejoin the flock as it moved on.[3]

Teaming is part of the postmodern "horizontal revolution" that is moving the fulcrums of power from machine based to people based, from pyramid to pancake, from ladder to web.[4] It is a "revolution" the church should be leading, not following, for we of faith are many, we are legion. It is in the Jesus genes and then in the Wesleyan genes to move from standing committees to moving teams. Teams, and their weavings into webs and networks and chords and partnerships, are part of the genetic hardwiring of the Wesleyan species.

The deployment of team culture in the core space from which disciples of Jesus live and move and have their being is one of the most necessary recapitulations of the Christian tradition that must be accomplished in the postmodern era. A team has been defined as "a small number [between two and twenty-five persons] of people with complementary skills who are committed to a common purpose, performance goals, and approach for which they hold themselves mutually accountable."[5]

A team does not simply replace or replicate what is already being done under the name of "committees"—the "HAMFAT ("Have a Meeting, Form a Team") syndrome." In fact, team leadership requires very different skills from hierarchical leadership. Team leaders need informal leadership masteries: the ability to bring out others' gifts, manage conflict, communicate strongly and clearly, build consensus, affirm diverse gifts. Team members also need to embrace multiple leadership roles that can only be grasped by many hands and many minds working together. In the star model of team leadership, there are key roles for an administrator (record-keeping), facilitator (processing meeting itself and group identity builder), coach (helping team members develop their skills and capabilities, and get training), workload coordinator, and external liaison (group communications).

Nothing is impossible . . . until it's sent to a committee.
Anonymous

Various kinds of teams are possible. "Work teams" or what I prefer to call "task teams" can do the core work of ministry, encompassing healing teams, visitation teams, cell groups, worship teams. "Integrating teams" make sure the various teams of the organism fit together; they help coordinate the efforts of the various teams, and keep the communication among all the teams high and free. "Management teams," like the board of trustees or the board of deacons, constitute a particular type of integrating team—in this case one that has a hierarchical role in the organism and is in some way accountable and authoritative for providing direction and evaluation to the rest of the teams. Improvement teams help upgrade the performance of the organism. Then there are R & D teams, problem-solving teams, project teams, generational teams, and so on.[6] The life cycle of teams also varies and resists standardization. Depending on the type, teams can be permanent or temporary, and the latter can be long-term or short-term. The board of trustees is most likely a permanent team; a project team (capital campaign, for example) is temporary.

85

I

Between Jesus' baptism and the arrest of John the Baptist, Jesus prepared for his ministry by calling forth in pairs some followers to be his team, and with them prepared himself mentally and spiritually for the challenges he was to face. With only three years in which to save the world, how did Jesus spend his time?

He invested everything he had in a team. No wonder Jesus became frustrated at times: "Have I been with you all this time . . . and you still do not know me?" (John 8:9). "How dull you are!" (that is, "Do you still not understand?" [Matthew 16:9 NIV]) "Do you also wish to go away?" (John 6:67). "Do you now get it?" (that is, "Have you understood all these things?" [Matthew 13:51 NIV]).

Net fishing is a team effort. The Bible knows nothing of solo ministry, only team ministry. The words "my ministry" ought never to leave the lips of a disciple of Jesus. Every ministry to which we are called is a ministry we do in partnership with others. This is what it means to be the body of Christ.

Ask not what your teammates can do for you. Ask what you can do for your teammates.

Magic Johnson

The Witness Principle is the teamwork ethic at work: You can't do it alone. "Where two or more are gathered together, there I am in the midst. . . ." Nothing exists in isolation: not atoms, not persons, not churches, not galaxies. Throughout the universe, God requires more than one "center." The Milky Way and the Andromeda galaxy anchor the Virgo cluster of galaxies. Throughout the Bible, God requires more than one witness to establish truth. Jesus is the first witness. The church, Christ's body on earth through time, is the second witness. Jesus said in the last days he would send prophets, sages, and scribes to proclaim his coming kingdom (Matthew 23:34).

God even reveals who God is through the witness teamplay of immanence and transcendence. In Genesis 1, God is the transcen-

86

dent God who speaks all things into being. In Genesis 2, God is the immanent God who sculpts us out of the earth itself. What is the doctrine of the Holy Trinity but an affirmation of teamwork? God is a Team: a harmonious interrelationship of unique persons—three in one and one in three. In fact, in his "that they all may be one" prayer in John 17, Jesus bases the unity of the human community on the "even as" unity of the Father and the Son—a unity that transcends rivalry and becomes "glory."

When one reads the Bible from this standpoint of teams, what one sees is amazing. The Bible is the story of collaborations—Moses and Aaron; Caleb and Joshua; Naomi and Ruth; Zerubbabel and Jeshua; Esther and Mordecai; Ezra and Nehemiah; Peter and John; Paul and Titus, Paul and Silas, Paul and Timothy, Paul and Epaphroditus, Paul and Onesmimus, Paul and Barnabas; Barnabas and Mark; Barnabas and Phoebe; Philologus and Julia; Mary and Martha.[7] Even the Gospels themselves are presented to us as a team—Matthew, Mark, Luke and John. God did not preserve Jesus' story with only one Gospel. Jesus' message and meaning are so complex and diverse that it takes four Gospels, four whole stories to give us the whole truth.

True quality requires heart, cross-boundary trust, and long-term relationships—the actual sources of new wealth.

Jessica Lipnack and Jeffrey Stamps[8]

When one reads the history of American evangelism from the standpoint of teams, what one discovers is that evangelists worked closely with musical leaders: Charles G. Finney and Thomas Hamilton; Dwight L. Moody and Ira Sankey; Billy Sunday and Homer Rodeheaver; Billy Graham and Cliff Barrows/George Beverly Shea (the former is seventy-three, the latter eighty-seven)—or increasingly, Michael W. Smith and DCTalk.

In the Wesleyan branch of the evangelical tradition, preaching itself was a tag-team match. First the circuit rider would provide the biblical exegesis exposition. Then the exhorter (sometimes lay, sometimes located elder) would bring the exegesis home. Finally, together they would work the altar.

In fact, Wesley designed the entire itinerant system as an enterprise in team ministry. In perhaps the most valuable of all Wesley's surviving autograph letters, he defends the itinerant system to Samuel Walker in these words: "I know, were I myself to preach one whole year in one place, I should preach both myself and most of my congregation asleep." Wesley went on to argue: "Nor can I believe it was ever the will of our Lord that any congregation should have one teacher only. We have found by long and constant experience that a frequent change of preachers is best."[9]

For me the word team *stands for Together Everyone Achieves More.*

West Virginia gymnast/
Olympic gold medalist Mary Lou Retton

If you're not a team player, you can't be a follower of Wesley, much less a disciple of Jesus the Christ. Jesus calls his disciples to join the real Dream Team.

Here is the logo of the Dream Team that began American Methodism.

88

Why have generations of ministers from the Peninsula Conference knelt on this star when they were ordained elder? Because here is the precise spot where the Methodist movement in America began. After Thomas Coke's sermon, the five-foot-nine-inch Francis Asbury stepped forward and hugged and kissed the five-foot-two-inch Coke. They then met and planned the formation of the Methodist movement. But the first thing they did was to draw in the talents and leadership of a third member of the Dream Team, someone named Harry Hosier.

From this one star, you can see the two major characteristics of a "Dream Team."

II

Dream Team Feature #1

The first feature of a Dream Team is "collaborative individualism."[10] Each of these leaders was an individual contributor/performer, even superstar, in his own right.

But at the same time, each of these "superstars" was a humble partner and team player, willing to take a backseat for the purpose of making the other teammates look good and do good. Hence the phrase "collaborative individualism." Or to use a formulation more common to the athletic world, each one was a breakthrough team player who was also an individual performer.[11]

Of the three superstars, Francis Asbury is the most familiar. Sent in 1771 by The Wesleyan Conference in London as a missionary to America, he quickly established himself as a leader of American Methodism. After their meeting on 14 November, Coke wrote in his journal:

> I exceedingly reverence Mr. *Asbury*; he has so much wisdom and consideration, so much meekness and love; and under all this, though hardly to be perceived, so much command and authority.[12]

Perhaps the next most familiar is Thomas Coke who was ordained an Anglican priest in 1772 and dismissed from his post in 1776 for conducting open-air and cottage services on the recommendation of Wesley. The following year he officially joined the Methodist movement and was named a superintendent of the new missions in North America by Wesley.

The least familiar, but in many ways the one with the largest mass following, was Harry Hosier, or "Black Harry" as he was known back then. Harry Hosier, one of the most gifted preachers in American history, often served as a teammate to Francis Asbury. He commanded vast audiences, and was present at the Christmas Conference.

While Asbury preached to the Whites, Hosier would preach to the Blacks. To Asbury's discomfort he often found his crowd migrating to the preaching of "Black Harry." After Asbury and Coke embraced, Asbury beckoned Hosier to come forward and meet with them. Coke needed a teammate to show him the way and ways of the Americans. Would he be willing to travel with Coke? Hosier agreed, and together the two of them traveled the countryside. Coke deemed him one of the finest preachers in the entire world.

Each of these three superstars was an empowered individual who had the freedom to act collaboratively. Each knew that he could not do it alone. But each knew that, working in collaboration with others, they could do something about anything. Asbury, Coke, and Hosier were proactive leaders who acted on and transformed the strategies, structures, and cultures of their day through loosely coupled empowered systems we today call "teams."

III

The guy who puts the ball through the hoop has ten hands.

Former UCLA coach
John Wooden

90

Dream Team Feature #2

The second feature of this Dream Team was "harmonious difference." The Dream Team Jesus puts together is not where like meets like, but where difference meets difference. Jesus exhibited a mosaic mentality. Look at the disciples. Here was a gloriously promiscuous mix of characters and talents, a team of difference.

Jesus picked a quiet/loud, passive/active, bold/shy, radical/conservative, lettered/unlettered, tough-minded/soft-touch, nice/belligerent bunch to be his Dream Team. In the divine mind there are many dwelling places, many cultures, many ecosystems. Jesus exhibited a mosaic mentality. A God who delights in diversity is evident even in the study of identical twins. Penelope Farmer's research into twins reveals that "there is no such thing as perfect doubleness. In the seemingly identical the differences are quite as significant—and in some ways more telling— than the likenesses."[13]

Or consider the lushness of creation itself. Variety is more than the spice of life. It is the very stuff of life itself. If there is one thing we can say with confidence about the Creator and the ten million species of life on this planet, it is this: God hates standardization; God loves variety. The more closely we zoom in on the molecular-genetic basis of life, the more we find differences and singularities and variations. The more we understand complexity theory, the more we find that life evolves variety, surprise, difference. The world produces itself as ever-different, never-same.

The God who calls us by name calls us to find ways of being different together. Pentecost reversed Babel, not through the creation of one language, but through the ability to acknowledge and affirm difference. When barriers come down, and a profusion of voices is allowed to sound, the result is harmonious difference. When God lets a thousand flowers bloom, and a thousand dialects be heard, why are we afraid around genuine diversity—whether it be ethnic or intellectual or spiritual? Why is it bad for the church to mean something different to each Christian? The greatest thing humans share in common is that we are all so different.

When Christians become more like Christ, they become more different from one another, not more alike. Francis Asbury, Thomas Coke, and Harry Hosier found in Christ the creative force to live more fully in their uniqueness. Novelist/lay theologian/rector's wife Sara

Maitland argues that Jesus' anthropology and ethics made difference a positive, not a negative.

> We are, quite simply, not "all the same underneath": a person as person is not androgynous, classless, colourless—nor, most importantly perhaps, timeless. Personhood, what it is to be a self . . . is to be created within particularity (within time and space). . . . Yet the scandal of particularity, the fact of the Incarnation, holds up difference, specificity, as desirable.[14]

The apostle Paul would be horrified by the homogeneity of our churches. He insisted that there were varieties of gifts, services, and activities, yet each one who worships would be given the "manifestation of the Spirit for the common good" (1 Corinthians 12:4-7). This is why large churches without small groups are utterly unbiblical. The bigger the church, the more indispensable the cells so that the distinguishing differences of authentic community can take place.

The early church was dominated, not by a single, unified thrust, but by a variety of leadership models and competing missions (such as Peter and James in Jerusalem, Paul in various other centers) that agreed on one thing: the centrality of Jesus the Christ.[15] The leadership in the early church was a network of teams. The Antioch Church, for example, was led by a leadership team of five who came from different backgrounds, even different countries (Acts 13:1). Paul's concern about the Corinthian church was precisely its lack of diversity. The church was dominated by a monoculture of spiritual gifts. Without genetic diversity, Paul argued, no organism (human body, Christbody) can be healthy. Diversity is an instrument for the "manifestation of the common good" (1 Corinthians 12:9). The body can't be healthy without diversity.

If you don't disagree with me, how will I know I'm right?

Sam Goldwyn

The genetics of genius were planted into the Methodist genes through its insistence on holding together a whole range of diverse elements within the Christian tradition. One historian (Albert Outler) calls Methodism an "ecumenical bridge tradition"; another scholar (Colin Williams) speaks of the "catholic synthesis" of the Wesleyan movement that held in harmony diverse tendencies within the Christian tradition. One biographer of Wesley even brought his divergent unities of head and heart together in the title: *Reasonable Enthusiast.*[16]

Methodists in America were multi-ethnic, multi-racial and gender-balanced (65 to 35 percent in favor of women, by the way) almost from day one. At the United Methodist Archives at Drew University, there is a large wall hanging that features *eight* maps of the U.S. on which are outlined the "Boundaries of Annual Conferences Methodist Episcopal Church, 1920)." There is one map of the U.S. with "White English-Speaking Conferences," including the "Norwegian and Danish work east of the Alleghenies, and all French, Spanish, Portuguese and Italian work outside of territory assigned to the Latin-American mission." There is another map of the "German Conferences," another of the "Swedish Conferences," another of the "Pacific Japanese Mission," another of the "Pacific Chinese Mission," a map of the Southwest with the "Latin-American Mission," a map of the "Norwegian and Danish Conferences" west of the Alleghenies. The "United" in the name "United Methodist" stands for more than the uniting of the German (Evangelical United Brethren) and Anglo (Methodist Episcopal/Methodist Protestant) sides of our heritage in 1968.

The second largest segment of that wall hanging was a map of the "Colored Conferences." In 1786, 17 percent of New York City Methodists were Black women, a figure that had climbed to 22 percent by 1795.[17] In 1794, St. George's Church in Philadelphia was 13 percent Black. By 1800, the two Methodist churches in Baltimore—Baltimore City and Fell's Point—were 36 and 26 percent Black respectively.[18] It would be hard to find a United Methodist, Baptist, or Presbyterian church today with that level of biracial congregational inclusiveness and cultural commerce. One social historian of southern evangelicalism argues that "of all radical changes of the Civil War and Reconstruction, the greatest in religious terms was the division of southern churches along racial lines."[19]

Differences are what make us indispensable to one another. Pentecost, the reversal of Babel, empowers us to recognize, respect

93

and respond to difference—not in the boring sense that "we are all alike" but in the baffling sense that "we are all in the same boat." Pentecost people interact and participate with people who are different from them. Pentecost people open their minds and hearts to people and practices that are different from their own. The Pentecost culture of the church sustains interactions with radical difference and cherishes a heterogeneity of modes of knowledge and interruptive experiences.

Whoever forms a team to carry out the best idea wins.
Laurie Beth Jones

Postmodern culture can rationalize diversity and imagination out of existence. The church has become too much like the rest of society—deeply ambivalent toward anyone or anything that is different. The peace we have made with difference—different color, class, nationality, gender, size—is an uneasy, unstable peace. We like knowing we are "right," and those different from us threaten our sense of "rightness."

There are 6,000 extant languages in the world; 3,000 are expected to disappear in the next century. A homogenizing monoculture of language is spreading over our planet like the homogenizing monoculture of grass. At the same time we need to learn the transnational languages of Chinese, Spanish, Russian, Hindi, English, we also need to protect and preserve the languages native to isolated people like the Ethiopian language of Gafat, spoken by less than thirty people and reduced even further when linguists, seeking to preserve it, transported two Gafat speakers outside the country who quickly caught cold and died.

To be sure, it often is not easy living in post-dialogue, post-diversity multilogue, multiverse communities. People fear and avoid community for good reasons. Workshop leader/sociologist Parker Palmer defines community as "that place where the person you least want to live with always lives." The subsidiary corollary to this definition is that "when that person [with whom you least want to live] moves

94

away, someone else arrives immediately to take his or her place."[20] Living in community requires so much forgiveness, endurance, compassion and participation it is little wonder many people prefer loneliness to relationship. Right now the business world may be teeming with teams, but many of these R&D teams, project teams, planning teams, quality teams, work teams are not working because either they are built on the assumption that people like working cooperatively, that teams are not trouble, or because teams are but a faddish name for committees.[21]

Diversity in the Wesleyan tradition emphasizes pluraformity over pluralism. In the former there are wide divergences around a common core; in the latter, there is no common core, and few connections. In pluraformity people embrace others, no matter how different, they listen to each others' stories, and they are open to others' perceptions without being empty of their own. In the apostle Paul's own words, without diversity none of us can be "mutually encouraged by one another's faith, both yours and mine" (Romans 1:12).

The important thing . . . is not so much to obtain new facts as to discover new ways of thinking about them.
Scientist W. L. Bragg[22]

Another reason why diversity is key to the Team Gene is because without diversity there is little creativity. Creativity is looking at everyday things differently, which means an openness to difference. Every major study of creativity boils down to this: new ideas come from the mixing of metaphors, the juxtaposition of difference, the jump-cutting of far-flung ideas. The openness of mind to odd and arbitrary associations characterizes the highly creative.[23]

One of the reasons eccentrics score higher levels of mental health in standard diagnostic tests is that they are much more creative than the general population. In the words of the researchers into eccentricity, "Original thinking, it seems, may be better for you than dull conformity."[24] The head of the MIT Media Lab, Nicholas Negroponte, sees difference as a key to choosing a vocation in the postmodern world: "My advice to graduates is to do anything except what you are trained for. Take that training to a place where it is out of place and stimulate ideas, shake up establishments, and don't take no for an answer."[25]

Want a creative team? Then mix fire and ice. Bring together people who have ages, cultures, disciplines, dispositions, and perspectives, that are as different as possible from each other. Make sure that in the mix there is a Brahma, a Vishnu, and a Shiva—a creator, a preserver, and a destroyer. Form cross-functional or cross-boundary teams that address problems less within areas than between areas—strategic alliances, virtual corporations, joint ventures, flexible networks, and the like. It takes the noisy, conflictive process of bringing diverse, even disparate, people together who see the world in different ways to generate new ideas. Instead of squelching annoying deviants and dissenters, "an authority should protect those whom he wants to silence."[26] Opportunity knocks more at the door of one's enemies than at the door of one's friends.

T. S. Eliot once defined "poetic originality" as the "assembling [of] the most disparate and unlikely material." "Com-posing" or "putting-together" is a workable definition of any kind of originality. The Center for Nanoscale Materials and Processing, headed by chemist Larry Dalton and Nobel Laureate George Olah, is composed of teams from a variety of diverse research universities across the country—Southern California, Cornell, North Carolina State, and others.

Fellers, I don't want you to feel bad about this. This has been a team effort. No one or two guys could have done all this.

Casey Stengel to his 1962 Mets upon losing a record 120 games

The bringing together of diverse work cultures is what made Vice-President Albert Gore's 1993 endeavor to "reinvent government" so pioneering. For the first time in history, he conducted a

National Performance Review (NPR) of the United States government, not utilizing outside consultants, or homogeneous teams of experts, but using two hundred insider bureaucrats who formed themselves into thirty-three cross-functional teams—one for each chief governmental department (twenty-two teams), and eleven agency-crossing "systems" teams that examined issues across departmental boundaries. The one rule was this: no agency team could be staffed by people from its own department.[27] Ironically, the worlds of money-making and movie-making are ahead of the world of soul-making in promoting collaborative enterprises, team efforts, and cross-functionality that bring together disparate groups.[28]

Methodists used to put on "singing schools" to help people learn to sing in harmony. Maybe the church needs to conduct "singing schools" as well as "diversity training" to teach people how to sing in harmony today. Maybe the church itself *is* the "singing school."

NetNotes

http://www.leonardsweet.com/netbooks /gateways/

Here you will find links to Chicago Bulls, Harry Hosier, T. S. Eliot, Billy Graham Ministries and various team related URLs. The Interactive page contains the "Matching Game" where you match team members. Selected images include Barratt's Chapel Asbury/Coke's Star, Francis Asbury, Thomas Coke, Harry Hosier and other team images. Your answers and comments about the "Rock-the-Cradle Discussion Questions and Activities" can be posted on the Gateways Forum under the Team Listing. The resources listing includes all indexed notes from the chapter, plus you can post additional resources under the Gateways Forum Team Listing.

Rock-the-Cradle Discussion Questions and Genogram Exercises

1. How does McDonald's get minimum-wage employees to work full-time when there is a vast shortage of labor for minimum wage jobs? They invite people to join "The McDonald's Team."

97

How well is your church doing at inviting people to "join the Jesus Team?"

2. Discuss why Billy Graham is now this nation's most respected citizen. Could it be because of the "Billy Graham Team?" From the very beginning, the "Billy Graham Team" pledged themselves to the "Modesto Manifesto"—a commitment to keep one another's feet to the fire to avoid those things that brought down the ministries of others—financial improprieties, sexual indiscretions, carping criticism of one another, ego exercises, and so forth.

3. How might the language of "teams" change your own church's vocabulary?

4. Does your church have teams of leaders facilitating people's spiritual journey?

5. Arrange a phone interview with Mike Foss of the Prince of Peace Lutheran Church in Burnsville, Minnesota, or Robert Lewis of the Fellowship Bible Church in Little Rock, Arkansas, two churches that are moving to a true team model of leadership.

6. Birders spend small fortunes in their desperate (and losing) attempts to outsmart squirrels and rid bird feeders of these "tree rats." An especially popular weight-sensitive feeder made by Century Tool & Manufacturing Co. (Cherry Valley, Illinois) is proudly named The Absolute. When it first came out five years ago, birders thought someone "had finally come up with the ultimate solution," says Sue Wells, director of the National Bird-Feeding Society. But in recent years, reports have surfaced that once again squirrels have defeated our most ingenious efforts—by teaming up with one another. While one squirrel stands on the counterweight bar behind the feeder, thereby keeping the front door from shutting, the other squirrel stands on the roost and feeds.

   Have someone bring in one of these feeders and discuss how teams work in nature as well as in church.

7. A recent study of The United Methodist Church argues that we are in decline partly because Methodism "has become middle-class" and has lacked "outreach to all sorts and conditions of persons. We have opted for a very narrow sociological group for our ministry and mission. There will be no recovery from decline unless we recover Wesley's missionary impulse to reach out and welcome all."[29] Do you agree?

98

8. To get your church to celebrate differences, why not send out some teams of "Noah's Doves" to visit other congregations and report back on what they saw and felt? Or ask your snowbirds to tell how the churches they are a part of in the winter months worship?

9. See how many "teams" you can identify in popular culture, e.g. Lone Ranger/Tonto; Batman/Robin/; Bonnie/Clyde; Luke Skywalker/Princess Leia; Butch Cassidy/Sundance Kid; Penn/Teller; Siskel/Ebert; Regis/Kathie Lee; Porter/Dolly; and so forth. What about three-or-more teams?

SIX

The GOOD (Get-Out-of-Doors) Gene

O let them be left, wildness and wet;
Long live the weeds and the wilderness yet.

Gerard Manley Hopkins[1]

In the fall of 1969, twenty college students set out in a yellow school bus/motor home/library for a year of accredited, multi-disciplinary education with wild America the classroom, textbook, and dormitory. The professor of this first-of-its-kind course, Project Nature Connect coordinator/director of the National Audubon Society Expedition Institute Michael J. Cohen, took them to a wilderness setting, got them out of the bus, and placed a thick mitten on one of their hands. He then set them loose to explore the natural setting—the wildflowers, the rocks, the plants, the wetlands—with their hands. He concluded the class by asking the students to "blow on their hands, kiss them, pinch them, sprinkle them with soil, cry on them."

Their homework assignment was to reflect on the explorations of the day. The essays were revealing: "The gloved hand was warmer and more protected, but it felt very little or not at all." Another: "It sensed things different than did the bare hand; it was numb to texture, form, motions, pain and touch."[2]

This one story has got our social and spiritual number about the world God created more than any other story of which I can think. We live mittened lives from the day we are born to the day we die. ninety-five percent of our short life is spent indoors. Beginning at age five, the state legally requires we spend 18,000 hours indoors in public schooling over the next thirteen years. Higher education is not grounded in any outdoor context of meaning and literacy.

We also live out of a mittened spirituality. Little daylight is allowed to penetrate the initiation into our spiritual inheritance as Christians. Look at the educational process of confirmands as they acquire the official culture of the church. It all takes place indoors. The church does not pride itself in the gospel's out-of-doors spirituality,[3] and there have been very few thunderbolts in the history of the church willing to cut through the fog laid about in the apparent service of maintaining the indoors dogma of the Christian church.

John Wesley was one of those thunderbolts. He tried to teach old dogmas some new tricks about the out-of-doors. In fact, he eventually came to see that Christianity perjures itself when it is anything less than an out-of-doors spirituality.[4] Wesley helped the church of his day get "down to earth," and showed eighteenth-century England how "down-to-earth" God's love for us is.

The early church was a product of the great outdoors. The contemporary church is a product of the not-so-great indoors. In the history of the church, "revivals" are nothing more or less than a means of getting the church back out-of-doors. Spiritual Awakenings are rediscoveries of Christianity's GOOD (Get-Out-Of-Doors) genes.

The Methodist movement got Christians to breathe the fresh air of the outdoors. In fact, one scholar warns "let it never be forgotten Methodism began as evangelism in the open air."[5] Less than a century later Evangelicals, United Brethren, and Methodists embraced and evolved camp-meetings because their forebears conducted "big meetings" and other services in barns, docks, fields, and streets. Methodists flocked to tabernacle revival meetings, which were held in open-air groves and brush harbors. Evangelicals and United Brethren were so "out-of-doors" that they were called "Bush Meeting" Dutch. Methodism was a GOOD faith, an out-of-doors religion.

The chapel that Phillip Barratt built in May of 1780 was built in the middle of a "dense primeval forest of gigantic oaks and pines," part of an eight-hundred-acre tract Barratt owned in Kent County.

The largest town (Dover, Delaware) was twelve miles away. The rectangular chapel was noted for what Methodists were noted for: plainness, simplicity, directness. What made it unusual was its windows. Here was a brick chapel not built in an urban center that had windows. And the windows opened the church to the out-of-doors. As one early writer put it, there are no "rich windows that exclude the light and passages that lead to nowhere."[6]

God sleeps in the minerals, awakens in plants, walks in the animals, and thinks in us.

Sanskrit proverb

Coke's journal entry for 14 November 1784 conveys a sense of early Methodism's out-of-doors spirituality:

> About ten o'clock we arrived at *Barratt's Chapel*, so called from the name of our friend that built it, and who went to heaven a few days ago. In this Chapel, in the midst of a forest, I had a noble congregation, to which I endeavoured to set forth our blessed Redeemer, as our Wisdom, Righteousness, Sanctification, and Redemption.[7]

How did five to six hundred people gather to hear Coke's four-point sermon in a place that could accommodate at most four hundred—and that's with everyone standing? A third of those who stood at the cradle of Methodism stood outside. They huddled outside the doors; they hovered around the windows. The walls of Methodist churches and chapels were porous.

Barratt's Chapel was in some ways the eighteenth-century equivalent of Thorncrown Chapel, located in Eureka Springs, Arkansas. Designed in 1980 by E. Fay Jones, an apprentice of Frank Lloyd Wright, it is perched on a steep slope in the Ozark Mountains nestled among oaks, maples, and dogwoods. When you enter Thorncrown, or when you worship at Barratt's Chapel, or when you attend a camp-meeting or quarterly conference, it is not so much that you've escaped from the elements as that you've entered a space where those elements become more intimate, charged and sacred.

What sense does it make to ask a society that discards its old people to save its old trees? What sense does it make to ask a society that regularly abuses its children to preserve the forest for our great, great grandchildren? What sense does it make to ask a government, which is continually preparing for war, to maintain the peacefulness of the natural world?"

Erstwhile professor/
forest activist Lou Gold[8]

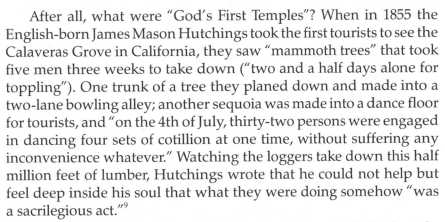

After all, what were "God's First Temples"? When in 1855 the English-born James Mason Hutchings took the first tourists to see the Calaveras Grove in California, they saw "mammoth trees" that took five men three weeks to take down ("two and a half days alone for toppling"). One trunk of a tree they planed down and made into a two-lane bowling alley; another sequoia was made into a dance floor for tourists, and "on the 4th of July, thirty-two persons were engaged in dancing four sets of cotillion at one time, without suffering any inconvenience whatever." Watching the loggers take down this half million feet of lumber, Hutchings wrote that he could not help but feel deep inside his soul that what they were doing somehow "was a sacrilegious act."[9]

Early Methodism rediscovered some ways in which the Jewish-Christian tradition engenders an eco-spirituality. In biblical Hebrew there is no word for "nature" for one simple reason. To talk about nature means that it is something separate from us. Psalm 148 portrays nature, not as something outside or opposed to us, but as something in which we are a part in a "great chain of being."[10]

With whom did God establish the covenant? Only with Noah? It was an ecological covenant that God made with "all flesh that is on the earth." (Genesis 9:16) That is why God kept sending Moses back in the negotiations with Pharaoh. Moses bargains out of Pharaoh, "Okay, the Israelite men can go and worship." But God said to and through Moses, "Not good enough. Let my people go." Moses demanded that "the people" be defined by Pharaoh as men, women and children. And not just for worship, either. For ever. But there is one final definition of "my people" that Pharaoh had to "get" before God was satisfied. This final, incredible declaration said it all: "Not a hoof shall be left behind" (Exodus 10:26).

When morning greets the skies . . .

Charles Wesley

John Wesley stood in a long line of animal sympathizers, including Pythagoras, Plutarch, Leonardo da Vinci, Thomas More, Montaigne, Jean Jacques Rousseau, Jeremy Bentham, George Bernard Shaw, Albert Schweitzer, and Mohandas Gandhi. Wesley is perhaps well-described as a creation theologian, the "deep ecologist" of the eighteenth-century church. His famous saying "Earn all you can, save all you can, give all you can" reveals a profound sense of the trusteeship of planet earth.[11] In one of his most neglected but prescient sermons entitled "The General Deliverance," Wesley's doctrine of creation linked the welfare of humans and animals together both in creation and fall.[12]

O God, my Master, should I gain the grace
To see you face to face, when life is ended,
Grant that a little dog, who once pretended
That I was God, may see me face to face.

French poet/novelist Francis Jammes[13]

In Wesley's later sermons on creation and new creation, the connections between theology and ecology become more explicit and integrated.[14] Every living creature has value in and of itself because God created it. If we take our wounds with us to heaven, why not our dogs and horses? Wesley understood how the Bible portrays the earth as morally sensitive—the ground throws up at

104

Cain's murder of Abel, the rocks cry out for Jesus on the cross when everyone else had abandoned him, are two examples. Often the earth and the animals that inhabit it are more morally sensitive than we humans ourselves. Revelation 11:18 even lists as one basis on which God will judge each person—how have you treated the earth?

Today we walk in the rainforest
Under its hangar of glass.

There is a device there now,
An electric clock whose numbers

Spin remorselessly. Time is
Burning backwards towards zero

As the forest shrinks in front of us,
An acre destroyed every second.

This leaflet in my hand
Might be all our biographies.

It tells of species that become extinct
Before they are discovered.

Robert Minhinnick[15]

Those who would blame the environmental degradation of our planet on the Christian faith are indulging in so much sixties nonsense. Exactly the opposite is the case: "The Bible is so detailed in its description of attitudes which should inform care of the earth that it has been likened to a 'manufacturer's handbook.' With this 'handbook' for operators, we have the instructions for smooth operation—but we have to follow them."[16] For Wesley the Bible taught that "some employments are absolutely and totally unhealthy—as those which imply the dealing much with arsenic or other equally hurtful

105

minerals, or the breathing an air tainted with steams of melting lead, which must at length destroy the firmest constitution."[17]

If anyone should be leading the charge against the four apocalyptic horsemen of species extinction—habitat reduction, pollution, over harvesting and the introduction of exotic species—it is Wesleyans. If our jeremiads don't work, perhaps satire will: Oh, please feel free to sacrifice other species for our selfish pleasure; feel free to treat any work of God with disregard and disdain; feel free to do whatever you want, not just with a single spotted owl or single redwood, but an entire ecosystem.

The whole landscape a manuscript
We had lost the skill to read.

John Montague[18]

It does not require membership in Mensa to figure out that the collapsing and unraveling of natural systems renders the protection of single species problematic. The church must move its concern from simply protecting single species to protecting whole ecosystems. Churchyards (along with hedges and meadows) used to be important ecosystem protections, unackowledged concessions and provisions Christians made to preserve wildflower and wild animal habitats. Two of the most endangered American systems, by the way, are the ones our zealous Wesleyan forebears were most responsible for cutting down: the midwestern prairie-savanna and the eastern forest. The two together covered 40 percent of what is now the U.S. before the Europeans arrived.

Ecopsychologist Theodore Roszak calls our lack of ethics about our planetary home "the epidemic psychosis of our time."[19] It is a "psychosis" most acute among the generation born before 1946, but it is a "psychosis" that is active and at work in every generation with perhaps the exception of the millennial generation. The environment is for most boomers a blind spot, their environmental consciousness often little more than a commitment to pretty pictures.

106

O God, enlarge within us the sense of fellowship with all living things, our brothers the animals to whom thou has given the earth as their home in common with us.

Basil the Great

Boomers are not tone deaf on this issue like their parents, but they are too self-absorbed to do anything about it. Increasing numbers of boomer home buyers are looking less at tennis courts, golf courses, and outdoor pools, and are wanting access to bike paths, hiking trails, and fitness centers.[20] But tree-hugging boomers have a need to prettify nature before they hug it, and end up often hugging nature to death. Boomers are quite willing to take bite-sized chunks out of mountains, or deserts, or whatever suits their fancy, to satisfy their spiritual and intellectual greening. Busters have a strong "ecological ego," a sense of ethical responsibility to nature, but are often too pessimistic and cynical to think that they can undo the damage done by their tone-deaf grandparents and tree-hugging parents.

Only the millennial generation, which has moved from their parents' preoccupation with "self-esteem" to "Earth-esteem," seems to understand the urgency for a greener spirituality conveyed in Roszak's conclusion: "A culture that can do so much to damage the planetary fabric that sustains it, yet continues along its course unimpeded, is mad with the madness of a deadly compulsion."[21] Only the millennial generation seems to grasp intuitively what the Bible communicates through the Greek work *Oikos*, which is the root for economy (*oikonomia*), ecumenic (*oikumene*), ecology and trustee (*oikonomos*). Economics, ecology, ecumenics, and ethics are all interrelated. In the powerful words of Larry Rasmussen: "Material and managerial well-being of the public household (*oikonomia*); the promotion of the unity of its family as a single family (*oikumene*); the knowledge of the envelope of life the household is part of, and dependent on (ecology), and the trusteeship of the household (*oik-*

107

onomos)—these are dimensions of a public vision of and for the church in our time."[22]

Dieter T. Hessel calls our "eco-justice" crisis the "pervasive new problem of our time," a "mega-reality" with which the entire church must come to terms.[23] The only way the church can do it is through what Hessel calls "trifocals"—to look at everything from its "below-abroad-outdoors" dimensions. The four ethical norms of eco-justice, as developed in a series of study books, are these:

1 **solidarity—value of community.**

2 **sustainability—social systems that are human scale.**

3 **sufficiency—distributive justice; redefinition of "good life."**

4 **participation—inclusion in the social process; inclusivity.**[24]

Jesus commanded his disciples to "Go into all the world [*cosmos*] and preach the good news to all *creation*" (Mark 16:15 NIV).

The church is the world's best hope to make "love of nature" and "love of neighbor" one and the same. Both the government and environmentalism have failed. Max Oelschlaeger, professor of philosophy and religious studies at the University of North Texas, calls the church to lead in caring for creation in these ringing words:

> The local church is a point of initiation for shaping voter preferences that lead to public policies addressing ecocrisis. The church is where individuals, caught up in the flow of their lives, in their joys and sorrows, can begin to grapple with the complexities of social existence. The church, in other words, is the natural home for dialogue that centers on creation, our place in the Creation, and our obligations to creation. The church is a place for conversation, where the faithful tell and retell stories that are emotionally evocative, psychologically persuasive, and ethically charged. Religious discourse can also lead individuals beyond the denomination or sect or mysticism toward conceptions of the public good. It is the church, in its function as a public church, that will help make environmentalism a reality. We should try to think of the public church as a coalescence among all traditions of faith on a common agenda to care for creation.[25]

NetNotes

http://www.leonardsweet.com/netbooks/gateways/

The GOOD Gene NetNotes contains links to National Audubon Society, Noah's Ark, Green Cross, UMC Rural Fellowship, Evangelical Environment Network, and various related URLs. The activities page contains the "Earth Pledge Exercise." Selected images include Barratt's Chapel with trees and other "outdoor" images. Your answers and comments about the "Rock-the-Cradle Discussion Questions and Genogram Exercises" can be posted on the Gateways Forum under the Good Listing. The resources listing include all indexed notes from the chapter, plus you can post additional resources under the Gateways Forum Good Listing.

Rock-the-Cradle Discussion Questions and Genogram Exercises

1. There is some evidence that environmental activism is becoming a spiritual discipline for increasing numbers of Christians. Listen to Amy Grant's rendition of Joni Mitchell's "Big Yellow Taxi" in her album *House of Love*.[26] Do you think this signals a new awakening to environmental issues among U.S. Christians in general and evangelicals in particular?
2. How hard is this statement for your group to affirm: pollution is blasphemy. During September of every year, would you feel comfortable praying for the healing of the ozone layer?
3. Does your church's "Stewardship Sunday" connect people to creation or separate people from creation? Is "Stewardship Sunday" about costly care for creation, or the cost of keeping church? Is it time to move beyond "stewardship" to something deeper? Would "trusteeship" be better or worse for defining the terms of Christian care for creation?
4. Should our environmental concerns be extended to gene pools as well as oceans and rain forests and rivers and forests? Aren't we at a place now where we can pillage and pollute the gene pool in much the same way our ancestors polluted the Great Lakes?

Is there someone in your church who can discuss issues related to genetic ecology?

5. Declare yourself an "Earth Steward" by learning and reciting "The Earth Pledge:"

I pledge to protect the earth,
And to respect the web of life upon it,
And to honor the dignity
of every member
Of our global family.
One planet, one people, one world,
in harmony,
With peace, justice, and freedom for all.[27]

6. Discuss the theological implications of this story: Once there was a man who was devout and religious and filled with thoughts of the Almighty. Each morning he would go to church, and so immersed was he in his devotions that he never noticed the children who would call out to him, or the wretched homeless who sometimes begged him for a coin or two. One day, he walked down the street in his customary manner, arrived at church, pushed on the door, but it would not open. He pushed again harder, and found the door locked. Not knowing what to do, he looked up and right before his face, he found a note pinned to the door. It said, "I'm out there."

7. "Is there such a thing," Wendell Berry asks, "as a Christian strip-mine?" What do you think?

8. The Church of the Messiah in Minneapolis, Minnesota, practices "vegetable evangelism." They engage kids in low-income neighborhoods of Minneapolis in gardening, and in so doing invite experiences and reflections on the meaning of creation, creativity, and spirituality.

9. Organizations/Resources you need to know about:

   a) National Religious Partnership on the Environment (NRPE)—Catholics, Jews, Mainline Protestants and Evangelicals joined together to address the spiritual roots of environmental concerns

   b) Evangelical Environmental Network (610-645-9392), and The Christian Society of the Green Cross (10 East Lancaster Avenue, Wynnewood, PA, 19096-3495; 1-800-650-6600).

c) Get a copy of a useful four-page guide to making your church more ecological entitled *Guide to Making Your Church a Creation Awareness Center* (order from United Methodist Rural Fellowship, 108 Balow Wynd, Columbia, MO 65203. Send $1 for postpaid copy)

10. Do you think that vehicles advertised as "off-road," expensive trucks that promise to plow over and through anything, will be attractive to busters and millennial kids who are deeply concerned about the environment? Is the future with Detroit's "Big Three"—which is investing heavily in expensive sport-utility vehicles, light trucks, and minivans? Or is the future with those German and European companies (Mercedes-Benz, Volkswagen, Renault, Fiat) that are investing in "micromobiles," eight-to-twelve-foot long smart cars with two to four seats, that are fuel efficient, safe, and cost about $10,000?

11. The Evangelical Environmental Network (EEN), founded in 1993 by Christian organizations committed to creation care, has provided an "Evangelical Kit for Caring for Creation," which has been used by over one thousand churches. Call 610-645-9392 for further information about this collection of resources.

12. Someone has observed that "Satan . . . is Nature: he has fur, horns, claws, scales, forked hoofs and a tail, he's found in the wilderness and he's seldom a white person." To what extent do you identify wilderness/nature as the enemy, as something to be "conquered" rather than celebrated?

13. Michael J. Cohen asks us to "Imagine a group of citizens, picnic baskets in hand, walking into a cathedral and chopping up the pews for firewood, roasting hot dogs on the holy candles, strewing litter throughout the sacred areas, carving graffiti, firing bullets and throwing hatchets into the columns, excreting in the holy water before washing their dishes in it, and then telling the Archbishop to clean up the mess. No citizen would do this, because the very nature of sacred places awakens senses that prevent this from happening. Even in war, we seldom bomb enemy cathedrals."[28]

Why is it so difficult for us to approach nature as a "sacred place" that must be treated with respect and reverence? Should we have more respect and reverence for our handiwork than God's?

111

FIVE

The *MINISTRY MOBILIZATION* Gene

Every baseball team, it is said, could use a player who plays every position perfectly. A player who never strikes out, who never makes an error. The problem is, how do you get that player to put down the hot dog and come out of the stands?

Methodism in America got bystanders to come down out of the stands and become players. Methodism began as a "lay" movement. It continued and grew as a partnership of "lay" and clergy leaders.

Mark Twain told the story of Captain Stormfield's visit to heaven, where he was shown around by an old bald-headed angel named Sandy McWilliams. To his surprise, when he asked Sandy who the greatest generals had been, Sandy replied

> Oh, a *lot* of people *we* never heard of before—the shoemaker and horse-doctor and knife-grinder kind. . . . The soldiership was in them, though they never had a chance to show it. . . . The greatest military genius our world ever produced was a bricklayer from somewhere back of Boston—died during the Revolution—by the name of Absalom Jones. Wherever he goes, crowds flock to see him. You see, everybody knows that if he had a chance he would have shown the world some generalship that would have made all generalship before look like child's play and 'prentice work. But he never got the chance.[1]

1

Lay Liberation

Methodism in America called forth laborers to become great generals. Laborers like "lay" preacher Richard Whatcoat, who became one of the great generals in the American church. Whatcoat was not ordained by the Church of England but was irregularly ordained a deacon and elder by John Wesley himself. Two months later, when he assisted Anglican priest Thomas Coke in the first communion ever conducted by American Methodists, he was only following in the footsteps of three "lay" predecessors—farmer Robert Strawbridge, carpenter Philip Embury, and soldier Captain Thomas Webb—whose plantings of Methodism in the colonies created strongholds of societies in New York City, Maryland, Virginia, and Philadelphia.

Most early United Brethren, Methodist, and Evangelical preachers were not ordained. Francis Asbury himself was not ordained until the Christmas Conference a month after the Barratt's Chapel meeting. In fact, "lay" preachers outnumbered ordained preachers by two to one through the 1820s. Most of the "ministry" (as we now would define it) was conducted in early Methodism by class leaders. Not until station appointments replaced the circuit did pastors begin to take over the pastoral duties of class leaders. The disappearance of the class-meeting in mid-nineteenth-century Methodism proved an acid bath for cell-group connectionalism regardless of class, gender, education, or economics.[2]

I baptized here about thirty or forty infants and seven adults. We had indeed a precious time at the baptism of the adults.

Thomas Coke[3]

The ambition of the Protestant Reformers was to create the first authentically "lay" piety. Martin Luther preached the doctrine of the

113

priesthood of all believers. But what did Luther and the others achieve? In Don Cupitt's words, the Reformation said to the "lay" person, "'You'll go on worshiping like a monk, only instead of looking up to the heavenly world you'll be taught to look up to your betters in general, and to the King in particular.'"[4]

It remained for John Wesley two centuries later to put the doctrine of the priesthood of all believers into genuine practice. No wonder some of our most fractious debates have been over the role and representation of the laity in church governance. Such polemics and pleadings are in our genes.

They're also in our general ecclesial genes. Think we're the first to have trouble figuring out our various roles in the body of Christ? Read Acts 6:2: "And the twelve called together the whole community of the disciples and said, 'It is not right that we should neglect the word of God in order to wait on tables. Therefore, friends, select from among yourselves seven men of good standing . . . while we . . . devote ourselves to prayer and to serving the word.'"

Wesley's mobilization of the laity was the hallmark of the Wesleyan movement. Susannah Wesley, the hand that rocked the cradle, was instrumental in convincing Wesley that the Great Commission must be fulfilled by "lay" people. It happened like this: When Wesley returned to London one day, he discovered that a layperson, Thomas Maxfield, not only had read Scripture in his absence, but expounded on the text. Wesley's Anglican blood boiled. But Susannah rose to Maxfield's defense, and after thinking about her words, Wesley expanded the use of the laity and the range of their ministry in the Wesleyan movement.[5]

What is amazing about Wesley is that he came to understand the vernacular faith systems of the people as not an inferior version of the faith of their social superiors, but as a faith system that had integrity in and of itself. In fact, if the truth be known, most of Wesley's most radical ideas and innovations he stole from the laity. Wesley was open to what he called "the leading of providence" and changed his strategies according to those leadings.

Some examples? A "lay" person, Captain Foy, came up with an idea for helping to pay off a debt that inspired Wesley to found the class meeting. A group of laity in Kingswood created services that went from evening until early morning, which led Wesley to form the tradition of Watch Night Services. The same story goes for the Love Feast, "lay" pastors, and much more.

Pastoring was done in early Methodism by the class leader, some of whom were women. Wesley was so open to the priesthood of all believers that he expanded the gender of "believers" to female as well as male. Wesley also inherited from his headstrong mother a commitment to strong leadership roles for women. Wesley was convinced by the preaching of Mary Bosanquet that women can communicate the gospel with as much anointing as men, and from 1771 extended his blessing to them. This commitment was picked up by the United Brethren and by the holiness and Pentecostal offshoots of the Wesleyan movement although it was not officially embraced by Methodism itself until 1956. America's feminist movements of the nineteenth and twentieth centuries found strong allies in Methodist circles. The rolls of the Wesleyan movement in all its variety and offspring included some of the most important names in the history of women's emancipation in the church.

After studying Wesley's ability to organize his "ministers" and deploy them in mission, the English historian/statesman Lord Macaulay once said that Wesley's genius for government was a match for that of Cardinal Richelieu:

> The genius of his organization is still seen in the church which he founded. It is owing to his superb executive ability and powers of organization that the movement remained unshaken even when deprived of his presence and guidance.
>
> His judgment of men, his skill in using them, his power to employ them to the best advantage and to attach them to himself in loyal submission to his authority amounted to genius and saved the movement from the most serious dangers.[6]

II

Give Away Ministry

Here is an exercise for your pastor to try out on the congregation. Have her ask for a show of hands as to how many present have been baptized. Then have her say: By the way, how many ministers are present with us this morning? The discrepancy between the two "shows of hands" is the extent to which your church is not living out of its "lay" liberation genes.

Or have your pastor try the same experiment with the term "call": How many present this morning have been "called" by God to enter ministry? Again, the "show" of hands reveals the extent of your church's problem in dealing with its own genetic makeup.

Contrary to what many Christians think, you don't need a graduate theological education to respond to a "call" to "ministry." The rite of "call" is baptism, not ordination. Every member is commissioned and installed by baptism to a "general office" of ministry, educated and equipped by those set apart for the "special office" of ministry.[7] Southern Baptist megachurch pastor Rick Warren is more Wesleyan than he cares to admit when he tells his people that the most important thing they may ever do with their lives is join Saddleback Church, choose a ministry, and serve Christ by serving others.[8]

The #5 gene uses with great difficulty the language of "lay" because this gene works to rid the body of this terminology of clergy and laity. The #5 gene purposively blurs the lines between laity and clergy. Wesleyans have always had difficulty around "ordination" precisely for this reason. Something special happens at "ordination," but we can't quite put our finger on what it is. "Ministry Study" commission after commission has failed to spell out precisely what difference ordination makes.

Just right. Bodies of Christ living out of their "lay" ministry genes will work to *abolish the laity*. An authentic Wesleyan church has no laity at all, only ministers. That is one reason why the language of "volunteerism" is such an abomination when used in the context of the church. Rotary recruits "volunteers." Kiwanis seeks "volunteers." The church of Jesus Christ deploys ministers. It is time to banish the language of volunteer from our vocabulary.[9]

What then does an ordained minister do? First, it is the "post-Jethro" ministry of the ordained (theologian Helmut Thielicke's concept) to *give up* the ministry: to educate and empower the baptized to offer their gifts to one another and the world, to delegate and *give away* ministry to others who then give away what they have to others, and to connect ministers to ministries, to connect passion to projects. The multiplication of ministries is the central leadership task of the church. In the words of one consultant, ordained leadership "is the development of laypeople who can minister the grace of God in its

116

many forms and, as a result, create obedient disciples of Jesus Christ who apply the truths of the Bible to their everyday lives."[10]

Second, an ordained minister leads from a spiritual pedestal that gives off a "right spirit" mystique that is healing and bonding. Perhaps an analogy from the medical world, one that struggles to come to terms with the doctor-patient relationship as a dialogue between experts, may help. Out of a long-standing tradition of doctor-writers (Somerset Maugham, Richard Selzer) and doctor-poets (William Carlos Williams in the U.S., Miroslav Holub in Czechoslovakia, Gottfried Benn in Germany, Rutger Kopland in Holland, Edward Lowbury in England, and others), the Welsh physician-poet Dannie Abse has some things to say about the mystique of the physician that has direct relevance to what "authority" is conferred upon ordination:

> The doctor needs to be, for the patient's sake, above the patient, a charismatic healer. However skeptical or sophisticated patients may be when they are healthy, a vestigial awe of the doctor-figure is precipitated when they are ill and should not be dissolved. Something primitive in us, deep down, leads us all to half-fancy that there are secrets in this world about healing that some doctors are privy to—secrets antecedent to all recorded history, and, in more recent times, translated into Latin and Greek from the hieroglyphs of a lost language. These secrets some doctors have in their possession—and if we know that this is not so when we are healthy, we may well think otherwise when we are stressfully ill. Then longing for a wizard, we send for his surrogate, the doctor, who bears no wand but a stethoscope and a prescription.
>
> Oliver Sachs is surely right when he declares, "There is, of course, an ordinary medicine, an everyday medicine, humdrum, prosaic, a medicine for stubbed toes, quinsies, bunions and boils; but all of us entertain the idea of *another* sort of medicine of a wholly different kind: something deeper, older, extraordinary, almost sacred, which will restore to us our lost health and wholeness." That other medicine is one of the secrets.
>
> One of my heroes knew that secret: Franz Anton Mesmer, Viennese physician and showman who carried a wand and wore a purple cloak. Mesmer claimed his healing power to be the result of "animal magnetism" which emanated from the stars and which he believed he had the gift to transmit. Mesmer had been trained as a doctor and was sincere in his beliefs; but he had the fringe-healer's intuitive understanding that showmanship and the awe inspired

by a reputation could heighten suggestibility and aid the healing process.[11]

The secret power of the ordained? Our secret power is our magnet spirituality—our magic touch of the Spirit, our overflow of soul energy.

Clergy are not going to "give up" the ministry without a fight, or "give away" their calling easily. One pastor wrote that this notion that he read about in the book *FaithQuakes*—that "ministry is not the clergy's job . . . [it] is the people's joy"[12]—was to his mind a "modern concept invented by people like Sweet" and others that is "unbiblical," contradicts "God's will," and would leave people like the apostle Paul "appalled" and "horrified." The Bible "knows" what "people like Sweet" don't know: that "laity have neither the time nor the training to accomplish ministry."

This pastor has lost touch with his "laity" even while he has got our number as "clergy." Millennium III is rightfully being called "the millennium of the laity."[13] The people, more information-rich than ever before, are more and more powerful. "The future will not be constructed," Jim Wallis argues, "from the mere shuffling of elite personnel at the top; rather, it will be a response to a transformation of values and action at the grassroots."[14] The postmodern church must build a diverse and dispersed leadership, which makes the reinvention of Wesley's and Asbury's partnership-model between "lay" and ordained leaders all the more inviting. True believers in the Wesleyan tradition don't "go to church"; we "gather as the church."

Matthew 10:24–33 makes it clear that it is not just some elite corps of "eyewitnesses" or "professionals" who are to declare the gospel "from the housetops." The task of "I-witnessing" belongs to all believers. It is long overdue to invite all of God's people to "come to the table"—not a "head table" that is square or rectangular, but a round table where "there are no sides." When the baptized discover what we the ordained have been keeping from them—when they experience for themselves how ministry gives us a "ringside" seat on the miracles of God—we will have to contend with a backlash of resentment, even anger, at what we have been hoarding for ourselves at the messianic table.

At a round table there are no sides, and all are invited to wholeness and to food. Roundtabling means no preferred seating, no first and last, no better, and no corners for "the least of these."[15]

Chuck Lathrop

III

Think Small, Think Complex

In Millennium II we learned to think big and think simple. In Millennium III we must learn to think small and think complex. Like a computer with parallel processors, instead of one CPU to do all the work (the clergy person), the church has multiple CPUs (liberated laity) not only to do the ministry, but to think it.[16] The business world is already complexifying and decentralizing its life by making work processes more and more horizontal and by weaning itself from bureaucratic pyramids and policies and hierarchical models. If you work at Disney, for example, you're not an employee, but a "cast member." Some airlines are training all employees to see themselves as salespersons. For no pay, and on their own time, airline employees can be found visiting local travel agents to "evangelize" for their airlines.[17]

Anglican Bishop Rowan Williams tells of remembering "someone saying about a mutual friend, a priest, who had great musical gifts, 'Perhaps he needs to discover his priesthood as a singer.'"[18] How many members of our churches need to discover their priesthood as cooks, as engineeers, as computer programmers? I ask churches with whom I consult "Who is your Minister of Food?" (never call them "caterers" or "directors of food service"). "Who is your Minister of Light?" (those in charge of overheads, projectors, etc.), "Who is your Minister of Sound?" "Who is your Minister of Photography?" "Who are your Ministers of Videography?" "Who is your Minister of . . . ?"

(Maintenance, Computer Services, Church Health, Communications, Singles, Congregational Care, Seekers, Choral Music, Imagination and the Arts, Liturgics, the opportunities abound).[19]

There is no area of church life where ministry cannot be exercised. The Bible mentions over twenty spiritual gifts in random, almost desultory order—as if these twenty "gifts" are meant to be suggestive of many, many more. Pittsburgh pastor Brian Bauknight plays a game in his church (he calls it a "spiritual exercise") called "gift bombardment." After a retreat or advance or prolonged time together, the group sits in a large circle. One person then walks to a chair in the center of the circle. Those on the perimeters then bombard that person with names of special gifts of God they have discovered in that person. This "gift bombardment" helps to celebrate that person's ministry in the body.[20] Other churches have different methods for calling out a spiritual gifts-based ministry for each member. One church puts its members through a two-day seminar where they discover their unique spiritual gifts. Then a "ministry consultant" works with each person to match their gifts to service in the church.[21] Through the seminary model of education proposed in this book, local churches become ministry empowerment zones.

But spiritual gifts are only one part of ministry in the Christbody community. Bruce Bugbee and Beth Lueders factor in "God-given passion and personal style" as supplemental avenues of service in their threefold approach to "Maximum Ministry."[22] In fact, our genetic endowment should make us nervous around exclusively gift-based ministries. After all, isn't the history of the church the story of God choosing people who weren't "gifted" to do what God called them to do? Doesn't God have a way of using people to do things who aren't "gifted" in doing those things?

How many biblical characters complained when called, "But God, I don't have a gift for this! I have neither the ability nor character to accomplish this task!" Take Moses, who protested God's call to lead the Israelites into the Promised Land, "Who am I, that I should go to Pharaoh and bring the Israelites out of Egypt?" (Exodus 3:11). Or take Jeremiah protesting his call, "Ah, Lord God! Truly I do not know how to speak, for I am only a boy" (Jeremiah 1:6).

There are sociological as well as historical reasons why gift-based ministries tell only part of the story. Peter F. Drucker argues that leadership is not born, it is learned. He argues that there is no "leadership personality," and no "leadership traits."

> Among the most effective leaders I have encountered and worked with in a half century, some locked themselves into their office, and others were ultra gregarious. Some (though not many) were "nice guys" and others were stern disciplinarians.[23]

Some were quick and intuitive, Drucker says, and others were cautious and studied. Some had instant intimacy; others were distant and aloof. Some were egotistical and vain; others were humble and self-effacing. Some were good listeners; others were loners and remote. There was one surprising thing all leaders had in common. They didn't have much "charisma."

Drucker says that the most effective leadership has four qualities:

1. The only definition of a *leader* is someone who has *followers*. . . .

2. An effective leader is not someone who is loved or admired. . . . . Popularity is not leadership. *Results* are.

3. Leaders are highly visible. They therefore set *examples*.

4. Leadership is not rank, privileges, titles, or money. It is *responsibility*.[24]

The greatest cause for pause around gift-based ministries, however, is theological. To be obsessed with giftedness while oblivious to godliness is to forget that I can't do it, that you can't do it. No matter how great your gifts, my training, your skills, my motivation, I can't do it and you can't do it . . . without God. Of course, God won't do it . . . without us. But through the power of the Spirit God can do in us and through us anything that God wants to be done.

For which is greater, the gift or the altar that makes the gift sacred?

Matthew 23:19b

Florence Foster Jenkins (1868–1944) was a wealthy New York socialite who hailed from Wilkes-Barre, Pennsylvania. For some reason she felt called to sing, even though she could hardly carry a tune, much less follow a beat. But because of this vision of her need to sing, she gave an annual private recital at the Ritz-Carlton Hotel and invited her friends to come to the party. Accompanied by pianist Cosme McMoon, Jenkins struggled through the standard operatic repertoire as well as the debuting of special songs McMoon had written expressly for her (for example, "Serenata Mexicano"). So famous were her parties, and so celebrated this eccentric woman who couldn't sing, that her tickets were harder to come by than a box at the Met on a Caruso night.

Jenkins had designer dresses made for her recitals, and she changed into at least three of them during the performance. One signature design was the "Angel of Inspiration" costume, which included full feathered wings. A taxicab accident in 1943 left her singing "a higher F than ever before" (only her listeners knew what she meant by that). Instead of suing the cab company she sent a box of cigars to the driver.

Her final appearance was her debut at Carnegie Hall. At the age of 76, she sang her favorites to a crowd that had sold out weeks in advance. A month later Jenkins died.

She wrote her own epitaph: "Some people say I cannot sing; but no one can say I didn't sing."[25]

NetNotes

http://www.leonardsweet.com/netbooks/gateways/

Included on this NetNotes are links to Martin Luther, Susannah Wesley, Carnegie Hall, Pope John Paul II, Leadership Training Network, Lay Ministries-related sites and ministry-related URLs. The Interactive page contains the "Spiritual Gifts Guide," which allows you to examine various spiritual gifts. Selected images include the Communion set in the Barratt's Chapel sanctuary and other ministry images. Your answers and comments about the "Rock-the-Cradle Discussion Questions and Genogram Exercises" can be posted on the Gateways Forum under the Ministry Mobilization Listing. The resources listing includes all indexed notes from the chapter, plus you can post additional resources under the Gateways Forum Ministry Mobilization Listing.

Rock-the-Cradle Discussion Questions and Genogram Exercises

1. Would you agree that we have become as a culture more "object oriented" than "people oriented"?

2. Get a copy of Pope John Paul II's 1991 *The Vocation and the Mission of the Lay Faithful in the Church and in the World* and use it for group discussion.[26]

3. It has been estimated that if each of ten thousand research scientists trained only ten research scientists in his or her lifetime, within five generations there would be one billion research scientists. Discuss the implications of this formula for evangelism.

4. Recommend here some Spiritual Gifts exercises. Use the resource book *What You Do Best in the Body of Christ*.[27]

5. Name the Ministers of Food in your congregation, and plan some kind of a celebration to thank them for their ministry in your midst. How does your church's Ministry of Food connect with what the World Bank in its *World Development Report 1990: Poverty* identifies as "the most urgent question" of the day: poverty?[28]

6. Have someone in your class read and review for the group Susie Stanley's "Empowered Foremothers: Wesleyan/Holiness Women Speak to Today's Christian Feminists."[29] Discuss Stanley's thesis that these Holiness and Nazarene women forebears of ours framed the issues of women's leadership in the church in ways strikingly similar to twentieth century feminists.

7. Attend a one-day forum on lay mobilization sponsored by the Leadership Training Network. Each person attending receives a *Starter Kit for Mobilizing Ministry*. For more information call 1-800-765-5323 or 903-561-0437.

8. Subscribe to *Into Action,* a quarterly newsletter published by Leadership Network for Directors of Lay Ministry and churches implementing lay ministry programs. It was released in August 1995. For more information call 1-800-765-5323 or 903-561-0437.

9. Discuss Kenneth Kinghorn's work on "Discovering Your Spiritual Gifts"[30] and his sixfold methodology:
   (1) open up to God
   (2) analyze your desires
   (3) examine your burdens

123

(4) evaluate your efforts
(5) focus on obedience
(6) watch how others respond

FOUR

The WIRED Gene

At Barratt's Chapel you'll find a mystery item. It was owned by Ezekiel Cooper, and he took it with him wherever he went. Some things he kept in it included writing implements, encryption devices (seal and wax), paper supplies, scales for weighing medicines, and so forth. Care to guess what it is?

That's right; it's a lap desk, and it contained a section that preachers like Cooper called a "Thunderbox," because it was here they stashed or filed their old sermon notes.

Does this circuit rider's "lap desk" remind you of anything? How about a laptop "'puter?" If there is to be a spiritual awakening in our tribe in the twenty-first century, we must learn to live out of our Wired genes. Our leaders must come to see themselves as electronic circuit riders.

A church that does not come to grips with technology is living in the death-grip of the past. God has a history of speaking through new media forms, beginning with the Christian church itself. Jesus came on the scene during a major technological shift: the transition from an oral to a written culture. It was difficult for some early Christians to come to terms with having the Gospels written down instead of circulated by word of mouth. The technology of writing violated the purity of word-of-mouth transmission. Yet the Christians were some of the first to claim this new technology and use it. In fact, the Christians invented the book. Whatever one thinks of the German scholar Carsten Peter Thiede's dating of three scraps of papyrus found in the library of Magdalen College, Oxford, containing fragments of Matthew's Gospel, his research does make it clear that Christians were the first to make the crucial transition from

125

writing on a scroll to writing on a codex—that is, what we now call a *book*.[1]

Fifteen hundred years later, a segment of the Christian community called Protestants was also the first to use another technology for the glory of God—the printing press. It wasn't easy to make this transition. Some who led the transition, like William Tyndale, were strangled at the stake, his body later burned. But thanks to these ancestors-martyrs, in the second half of the sixteenth century, with only six million people and limited literacy, over five hundred thousand vernacular Bibles were sold in England. Had the Protestant reformers not provided the impetus, would a vernacular Bible have been issued? I don't think so.[2]

Today we are being asked to do what our ancestors did before us: bring the church into a new technological world. In a sense, of course, every generation has to answer the same question: How do we exploit technology without letting it ensnare or enslave us? (There is now Communications Anonymous or "CA" for people inordinately attached to their communications technology—cellular phones, beepers, faxes, car phones, multiple phone lines, e-mail, voice mail, call return, and whatever else may become available.)

Technology is the campfire around which we tell our stories.
Electronic Music Composer Laurie Anderson

Methodism's historic openness to scientific and technological developments is one of the distinguishing features of the movement. Historian D. W. Bebbington has demonstrated the degree to which early evangelicals in general and Wesleyans in particular subscribed to the scientific method, touted "experimental religion," wrote scientific treatises called "Enquiries," brought science and theology together, and generally ushered orthodox Christian faith into the new world of the Enlightenment.[3] In the last decades of the nineteenth century, Methodists eagerly came to terms with Industrial Age technologies like the telegraph, typewriter, mimeo machine, and filing cabinet.

Both Wesley brothers bridged to the common people the arts and sciences of high culture through lyrics steeped in the literature of the English, Latin and Greek languages, hymns that brought the Scriptures to bear on everyday problems illumined by science and technology.[4]

John Wesley's ability to keep up with the scientific advancements of his day was amazing. His belief and use of the scientific method made him an "early adopter" of such technologies as electricity, which Wesley experimented with as a healing device, and mass printing, which Wesley positioned for the education of the poor. Wesley even invented a special reading chair that enabled him to sit backward, lean forward, hold the book sideways, and take notes on a built-in lectern while reading.[5]

Wesley was not alone in being known as an early adopter. Isaac Watts, best known today as a hymn writer, was more famous during his lifetime for his scientific pursuits.

John Wesley invented the religious paperback in the eighteenth century. His listing of thirty paperbacks in "A Plan of the Society instituted in January, 1782, to distribute religious Tracts among the Poor," a flyer that was bound with Wesley's 1784 *Arminian Magazine* (volume 7), stands as the earliest paperback list on record.

Wesley's mind was stored with and his theology shaped by the leading-edge scientific thinking of his day. Like the Protestant Reformers before him (especially John Calvin), Wesley insisted that Christians take the sciences seriously, and develop their knowledge in all areas of academic pursuit. He read new books on science almost as fast as he read theology texts, devoting one day a week for the study of metaphysics and science. While his colleagues and contemporaries were denouncing scientists like Sir Isaac Newton, who was anti-Trinitarian and associated with John Toland (the man who invented the term "pantheism"), Wesley used the hardest thinking of his day as the surface against which to press his mind—as if the mental and spiritual engagement with the most cutting edges of science and technology were a battery of mental and spiritual isometric exercises. For this reason Wesley read and summarized the thinking of biologists/naturalists (Bonnet, Buffon, Linnaeus, Lamarck, Cuvier), philosophers (Locke, Berkeley, Butler, Leibnitz, Hume, Kant), mathematicians (Barrows, Newton), astronomers (Halley, Kepler).

Wesley didn't always agree with these leading-edge thinkers. His citations of Newton were almost always critical. Nor did Wesley yoke religious faith to scientific findings, a surefire receipe for obsolesence. But he constructed the containers for theological content out of the categories and patterns of his day. In fact, based on these readings, Wesley summarized the most cutting edge scientific thought of his day for the common people in such publications as *Survey of the Wisdom of God in Creation; or, A Compendium of Natural Philosophy* (1763).[6] Scientific literacy was such an important tool to the trade of ministry that Wesley advised clergy, in this communication dated 6 February 1756:

> Some knowledge of the sciences also, is, to say the least, equally expedient, nay, may we not say, that the knowledge of one (whether art or science), although now quite unfashionable, is even necessary next, and in order to, the knowledge of the Scripture itself?
>
> Should not a minister be acquainted too, with at least the general grounds of natural philosophy? . . . Assisted by this, he may himself comprehend . . . how the invisible things of God are seen from the creation of the world; how the "heavens declare the glory of God, and the firmament showeth his handiwork."[7]

Little wonder when Wesley was asked the requirements for ministry, he replied that one question every minister should ask himself is "Have I mastered Gravesande, Keill, Sir Isaac Newton's *Principia* with his 'Theory of Light and Colours'? In order thereto have I laid in some stock of mathematical knowledge?"[8]

Wesley himself used Newton's law of gravity in a sermon (dated 1730),[9] although there is the comforting evidence for those of us today who are trying to grasp quantum mechanics and complexity theory that the bulk of Wesley's understanding of Newton came from secondary sources. Wesley, while he celebrated the Enlightenment's scientific achievements, argued with much of its theological implications. He thought, for example, that Newton removed God too far from everyday life, even though Newton didn't remove God as far as the Deists and their clockmaker God.

I

It's time for the Millennium III/Century 21 church to become a church that is agile, virtual, global with cybernetic methods of communications. In short, it's time we got wired, we got humming. If you can't hear the hummmmmm, your church is living in the wrong century. In fact, right now if we were living out of our #4 gene we would be preparing to go wireless.

Computers are useless. They can only give you answers.

Pablo Picasso[10]

Instead, we're watching others take the lead. The Buddhists are on-line. Buddhists have bought their own satellite in Japan. The Muslims are on-line. The Muslims are buying satellites all over the world. The Roman Catholic Church has taken up residence on the World Wide Web. They are sending missionaries into cyberspace, and have their own "home page" on the Internet. Known as "Catholic Online," the CompuServe system went up in February 1996. A fourteen-year-old boy is the "host" of one of its forums. You can download items from a 30,000-document library, talk to a priest online, or chat with other Catholic singles.[11]

You will even discover that the Benedictine monks are on-line. The Monastery of Christ in the Desert outside of Abiquiu, New Mexico, hooked up to the Web by a cellular phone which is powered by solar energy, boasts "the most beautiful Web Site on the Internet" (www.christdesert.org/pax.html).[12] Along with more than eighteen monastic communities around the country which together form the Electronic Scriptorium, these monks have a new "cybervocation," as they call it. Clad in hoods and blue jeans, they no longer make rosaries and crafts to sell in gift shops. Instead, they support their order by designing computer pages for the Web, working on computers, and similar electronic projects. "We've been making pages for 1500 years," reads their ads.[13]

Part of what we're doing in using computers is to prove in some tiny way that you can use modern technology and not be dehumanized by it, not lose one's soul. The information revolution can be a humanizing force.

Brother Patrick Creeden
of the Monks of Jerusalem[14]

Even the Amish are on the Internet. They have a home page in cyberspace called "Ask the Amish." It is a part of the World Wide Web site called the Pennsylvania Dutch Country Information Center. If you go to http://www.welcome.com/, and click on "Ask the Amish," someone brings your questions to the Amish/Mennonites, who either write the answers by hand or, in the case of the Mennonites, type the answers, which then are e-mailed to the person who asks the question.

Where is your church? In the know, or out of it? Smart and cybersavvy, or clueless and cyberklutzy? Instead of leading the way in showing how electronic technology can be used faithfully for the glory of God, mainline churches are like deer crossing the road, frozen in the headlights, absolutely paralyzed by the onrushing technology, wondering why we are being clobbered and cast to the side of the information superhighway.

The invention of electronics will be as significant to planet earth as the discovery of fire or the invention of the wheel. A remote control unit is the electronic age equivalent of the stone axe. Using the Net today is like turning the crank on the early automobile. Think how frustrating it was for our ancestors turning those cranks and constantly stalling out. The first automobile in the U.S. didn't get 90 feet before its transmission blew. Our children and grandchildren will one day ask us: "You mean you really typed in all that 'http://www.com' stuff?" Electronics is one place where we need to sit at the feet of our children. Michael Simmons, CEO of Dataport Computer Services, founded the telecommunications company at age twelve.

There are children playing in the street who could solve some of my top problems in physics, because they have modes of sensory perception that I lost long ago.

J. Robert Oppenheimer

Already video, phone, and computer technologies are cross-pollinating to give us something totally new (some call it "compuphonavision"—no word that awful has any future for itself, but I mention it anyway). Mix together the information superhighway, five hundred-channel televisions, set-top boxes, multimedia, wireless communication, palmtop computers, digital technology, and what do you get? Even netnauts don't even know what to call it other than MEGAMEDIA.[15] One of Bill Gates's pet ideas is a wallet PC that will hold electronic money, credit cards, digital plane tickets, photos, addresses, and other personal documentation.

We used to debate the number of angels that could dance on the head of a pin. Now it's the number of bits and bites. Today's common Pentium workstation is four times more powerful than the mainframes that put a spacecraft on the moon in 1969.[16] Scientists are now working on what they call "quantum computers" where information is stored on atoms themselves. If each atom could store one bit of information, a single grain of salt could contain as much information as the RAM in all the computers in the world.[17] The linking of genetics and computers, the human brain and computers called "wetware," and the notion that the computer could be connected directly to your brain, able to read your thoughts and waves (virtual telepathy) is no longer science fiction. The cutting edge is being done as scientists help the disabled lead better lives by devising mechanisms by which the computer translates electrical signals generated by the nervous system into patterns that can be interpreted and passed on.

The issue here for our tribe is more than building a home page on the World Wide Web (do you have one? who is your PageMaster?) or buying computers for offices (how many does your church have?)

131

or using computers in classrooms (a U.S. Department of Education survey found that, alas, there was only one technology essential to the public classroom—a photocopier) or instructing architects to design "smart" churches that are electronified (does your education area have a computer lab where electronic instruction can take place?).

The issue is larger than computers. After all, computers are old-hat. Have you heard about the kid, looking at a typewriter, who says: "Hey, there's a printer with a keyboard"? (Reminds me of another kid who announced to his teacher "My mother doesn't buy food; she buys ingredients").

The issue here for our tribe is a communications revolution that revolves around the culture of the screen instead of the culture of the book. Our tribe is in the digital dark ages; our tribe is at the bottom of the information food chain. Why does our tribe have to be a creative debtor, an idea debtor, instead of a creative creditor for this Information Age? In the words of Bill Waldrop,

> The information revolution has come to the churches. It has already created two classes of churches: those that continuously acquire and use the latest and best information they can get and those that do not. Consequently, what we see are churches that are either on the cutting edge in the way they view missions or churches that are doing mission much as it was done in the 1950s or 1960s.[18]

If our tribe recontextualizes its ministry in terms of an electronic culture, we must do more than broadcast our worship services—which in some ways is like the Encyclopedia Britannica's decision, in its pursuit of getting all the volumes onto one CD-ROM, to take out all the maps and pictures and graphs.

For the Christian church to deconstruct its print culture ministry and recontextualize its ministry for an electronic culture, the church must come to terms with the collapse of space and time.

II

In an electronic culture, any place can become every place. Technology redefines distance: emotional, social and psychological distance as well as economic and social distance. Distances are no longer barriers between people; boundaries (whether natural or national) no longer keep people apart. Indeed, distance is dead,[19] although location is more alive than ever before. It costs as much now to call a person in London, as it does to call the person next door. In the remote Russian province of Tuva, which borders Mongolia, herdsmen promote their haunting "throat singing" rituals on the Internet.

Or to take an example closer to home, one of the most rural and remote states in the U.S.—Iowa—has become "The Smart State for Business." Why? It is the first in the nation to install a fiber-optic telecommunications system (at a cost of one hundred million dollars) that puts every Iowan within a twenty-minute drive of an end-use site at educational institutions in each of Iowa's ninety-nine counties. In other words, Iowans are already doing video conference lectures, accessing on-line libraries, and in-person discussion groups. Iowa may now be the most accessible place in the nation.

The demise of distance . . . may well prove the most significant economic force shaping the next half century.
Editors of *The Economist*[20]

Similarly, an electronic culture sounds the death knell to issues of time. Time is near dead. Americans' love affair with VCRs and video (between 1988 and 1995 home video watching alone went from thirty-five to fifty-four hours annually) is partly due to their freeing us from the constraints of time. Through what is called "time shifting" active adults can tape TV shows to watch at their leisure, or wait for the movies to come out on video.

When Americans go on-line what do they do? Do they engage in "information retrieval"? Yes, many do, as *Christianity Today* found out when it first went on America Online (AOL). Its most optimistic projections estimated 60,000 dial-ins for information. *Christianity Today On-Line* actually got 600,000 "hits," as it almost overnight became, for a while, the most widely used segment of AOL.

But even more than "information retrieval," most people get online to engage in "community"—by a 60:40 percentage ratio ac-

133

cording to Steve Case, the CEO of America Online.[21] The "community" being formed on-line is asynchronous, with issues of time—"be there at 7 p.m."—no longer relevant. United Methodist layperson John Hendricks, founder and president of the Discovery Channel, has introduced "Your Choice TV" whereby anyone can order any episode of any TV program within a week of its showing for a small fee. In his words, "Television has always been appointment viewing, and someone else was setting the appointment. In the future, the viewer will set the appointment," argues Hendricks. On-line, asynchronous worship (worship in a twenty-four-hour church as one logs-on and joins in anytime night or day) is already a feature of many electronic Bulletin Boards.

The art of letters will come to an end before AD 2000. . . . It shall survive as a curiosity.

Ezra Pound

If we live out of our Wired genes, and become "as wise as serpents/as innocent as doves," our tribe has little to fear from this Information Era. In fact, one of the most interesting features of the culture of the screen is the way it recapitulates the past and brings the ancient into the future. The McLuhan Theorem is right: innovations in new medium are always revivals of old media.

- Who would ever have imagined that the emerging electronic technologies—modems, e-mail, the Net, the Web, fax machines ("faxcess")—would be writing based and indeed would bring back the lost art of letter-writing?
- Who would ever have predicted that the electronic era would bring back the literary arts (poetry, prose, and other literary forms)?
- Who would ever have predicted that 900 numbers would bring back the party line?
- Who would ever have predicted that the more sophisticated technology gets, the more important the arts become (computers make it easier to be a musician and make it easier on

134

dancers—colors for movements, lines for stage direction, shapes for interpretation; once the choice for artists was only oil and watercolor; now the choices are hundreds)?

- Who would ever have predicted that the most watched musical event in history to date is the 1994 televised concert of "The Three Tenors" (José Carreras, Luciano Pavarotti, Placido Domingo)?
- Who would have ever imagined that electronics would bring back family ties and family feeling—with parents more accessible to their children?
- Who would ever have guessed that an electronic culture would bring back a hunting and gathering economy, with the future belonging to the independent contractor, the freelancer, the self-employed?
- Who would ever have guessed that an electronic culture would bring back the Shakespearean art of drama, with one of the most important staff members any church can have being the Minister of Script writing and Minister of Drama?
- Who would ever have guessed that an electronic culture would put parents back in the home, not take them out of it?
- Who would ever have guessed that millennial kids are more likely to listen to the old-fashioned media called radio (which Marshall McLuhan called "the tribal drum" because of its ability to stir primal emotions—Hitler was the product of radio) than play high-tech video games; kids' radio is mushrooming—for example, the eighteen-hour-a-day Seattle station called "Kid Star" (KKDZ-AM)
- Who would ever have predicted that in an electronic culture Americans would continue to spend more on books than on any other kind of entertainment (23.8 billion dollars in 1994—more than subscription TV, home video, recorded music, daily newspapers, consumer magazines, cinema, and home video games)?
- Who would ever have guessed that in a culture of the screen the technology of print would be the best launchpad for new ideas or a political career (Colin Powell) or even understanding electronics itself (*Wired, 21c,* to name but two new titles)?
- Who would ever have predicted that an electronic culture would bring back the milkman and the storage box that opens from both the inside of the house and the outside—a refriger-

135

ated space in which grocery stores and gourmet food services will deliver food that you've ordered on-line when you're not at home?

- Who would ever have predicted that the weapons of the future would be transistor tape recorder, which helped over- throw the Shah of Iran (by bringing to the people the speeches of the Ayatollah Khomeini), the computer, which led to the fall of the Soviet Union, and the fax machine, which fueled the rebel cause at the Tienanmen Square uprising in 1989?
- Who would ever have predicted that the postmodern quest for higher modes of consciousness would lead to a poetry boom unlike any we have seen for centuries; we are now in a golden age of religious poetry, and have a poet for a pope.
- Who would ever have imagined that magazines like *Wired*, *Hotwired*, and *21c* would so bring together word and image, the textual and the pictorial, that they would recreate the pinnacle of artistic achievement in the early Middle Ages, the illuminated gospel books?
- Who would ever have imagined that an electronic culture would move church musicians from staff performers to resi- dent poets?
- Who would ever have imagined that this Rambo-ridden, Tar- antino-violent culture would have rushed to pick from the library shelves bankable literary classics to throw on the screen like *Persuasion*, *Pride and Prejudice*, and *Sense and Sensibility*?
- Who would ever have imagined that an electronic culture would have brought back into fashion books of fine binding, with elaborate gilt tooling of interlacing patterns, colored in- lays, painted strap work, and the like.?

NetNotes
http://www.leonardsweet.com/netbooks /gateways/

The Wired Gene NetNotes contains links to William Tyndale, Sir Isaac Newton, Pablo Picasso, The Monastery of Christ, Amish-related sites, AOL Web site, WebTV and *Wired* magazine and other wired-related URLs. The Interactive page contains the "10 Commandments of Postmodern Architecture," which allows you to do your own Top

10 List. Selected images include the Lapdesk of Cooper, which looks remarkably like a notebook computer and other wired images. Your answers and comments about the "Rock-the-Cradle Discussion Questions and Activities" can be posted on the Gateways Forum under the Wired Listing. The resources listing includes all indexed notes from the chapter, plus you can post additional resources under the Gateways Forum Wired Listing.

Rock-the-Cradle Discussion Questions and Genogram Exercises

1. Bring to cell meeting a copy of *Wired* magazine, and the children's book *The Magic School Bus in the Time of the Dinosaurs*.[22] Witness first hand and discuss how kids are now no longer reading in simply linear fashion. Share how it feels for a Gutenberg person to read a post-Gutenberg children's book printed like an electronic hypertext?

2. Demonstrate to the group some sampling of new ways of reading the Bible—not with bookmarks and paperweights, but with multiple on-screen windows and electronic bookmarks. "Show and Tell" to the group these electronic resources:

Mac Resources:

a. *MacBible* (Zondervan)—New Revised Standard Version, New International Version and New International Version Study Bible Notes in three windows (simultaneously or scrollably)—you can get add-ons of King James Version, New American Standard Bible, New American Bible, Hebrew Old Testament, Greek New Testament, and others)

b. WORDSearch (NavPress)—electronic concordance; get *Strong's Concordance* as an add-on

c. BibleMaster (Lockman Foundation)

d. *Thompson Chain HyperBible*—(Kirkbride Technologies)—hypercard based program (now on CD-ROM)—includes six major English translations of the Bible

137

e. *Online Bible* (for Mac)—largest collection of English and foreign-language translations and commentary modules around

f. *acCordance* (GRAMCORD Institute and OakTree Software)—Mac only: more serious Bible students; you can generate from this maps, charts, graphs, tablers, and so forth. Easy to use for anyone who knows Greek or Hebrew

Windows Resources:

a. *BibleSource* (Zondervan New Media)—text searches, note-taking, multiple English language translations available

b. *Online Bible*—same as Mac version

c. *BibleMaster*—same as Mac version

d. *Thompson Chain HyperBible*—same as Mac version

e. *GRAMCORD for Windows*—attached to *SeedMaster*, with all the things in *acCordance* mentioned above

f. *BibleWorks for Windows*—most serious resource; includes over thirty Bibles and reference works

g. *New Bible Library CD-ROM* (Ellis Enterprises)—twelve English Bible translations

h. *PC Study Bible* (BibleSoft)—best designed for Bible-study or Sunday school lessons; user-friendly

i. *Logos Bible Study 2.0* (Logos Research Systems)

j. *Bible Windows* (Silver Mountain)—best for serious students and pastors

3. Arrange a telephone interview during your class time with a postmodern circuit rider like Carol Childress of Leadership Network.

4. Billy Graham pushed his people to launch a worldwide satellite mission ten years ago (Global Mission was finally launched in 1995). Graham believes the church is twenty years behind the rest of society in claiming an electronic culture for Christ. Is he right? To what extent has Graham's ministry lived out of the Wired genes?

5. At Central United Methodist Church in Albuquerque, New Mexico, there is a stained-glass window that has in it a typewriter and

a wastepaper basket. Pretend you are commissioning a new stained-glass window for your sanctuary. Discuss how different generations might react to the possible presence in stained-glass of a computer or WebTV.

6. Discuss ways your church might supplement on-site education with on-line learning.

7. Select someone from your congregation to be one Sunday the church's Minister of Videography or Minister of Photography. Give them their first project of presenting pictures on screen to the congregation of what the minister is praying for—for example the courthouse, the leaky roof, Aunt Mildred who is going in for surgery, and so forth.

8. How well is your church at implementing what I call the 10 Commandments of Postmodern Architecture, which are as follows:

   10. Thou shalt not make any graven images.
   "You are building sacred space; design for multiple use and re-cycling of the facilities. This new world is one of change and complexity, not stability and order."

   9. Thou shalt not commit an ugly.
   "Your job is to put people in places of beauty, not indulgence. Aesthetics has everything to do with soul-making."

   8. Thou shalt not design for one sense alone, but all five.
   "You must design space that engages all five senses . . . consider them as a whole, not in isolation from one another. Smell will be the most important sense in the 21st century."

   7. Thou shalt have a sense of place.
   "People today more than ever need roots, a place of belonging. Design for the culture that God has given us and increasingly, ours is an electronic culture and that means screens, especially in the learning space of a church."

   6. Thou shalt get real.
   "The post modern church is reality based, not performance based, and uncovers hypocrisy. Design for interactivity and accentuate people's relationships."

139

5. **Thou shalt build an organic, living church**.
"The emphasis in the future will be on arches, domes, and atriums, not glass, steel, and sealed windows."

4. **Thou shalt take the church out of doors.**
"Christianity is an out of door religion. Pay attention to gardens outside and 'sky gardens' inside."

3. **Thou shalt love the land on which you stand.**
"Be environmentally responsible."

2. **Thou shalt not build dumb buildings.**
"Build smart churches that can glorify God."

1. **Thou shalt build spaces in which people can experience God.**
"Point people to something larger than themselves. Build the sky in which souls may soar."[23]

THREE

The HEALTH & HOLINESS Gene

The hero in Evelyn Waugh's novel *Vile Bodies* (1930) endures a screening shown at his future father-in-law's house of a Hollywoodish historical film about the life of John Wesley (*A Brand From the Burning*). A scene vividly portrayed in the movie shows Wesley, captured by Native Americans in Georgia, tied to a totem pole and about to be scalped. Suddenly his patron, the Countess of Huntington, comes riding on the scene, disguised as a cowboy. She unties him and throws him across her saddle. Together they ride off to safety.

The local rector remarks: "I had no idea Wesley's life was so full of adventure."[1]

The vicar didn't know the half of it.

For John Wesley, however, the adventure was all for nought without the holiness gene. At the heart and soul of the Wesleyan movement was this call to holiness, or what Wesley often called his doctrine of "perfect love." Wesley called the holiness gene "the grand depositum," the very reason God raised up the people called Methodist in the first place.[2] To this day, no United Methodist minister ever gets past the question: "Are you going on to perfection?"

Wesley's response to those who balked at these words was, "Well, if not that, then what? Are you then going on to imperfection?" The holiness gene makes the life of faith a lifelong growth in grace and in the knowledge of our Lord and Savior Jesus Christ.

Wesley's other great fear besides the fact that his descendants would abandon holiness was that people would misunderstand what he meant by the term—even people as close to him as his brother Charles and George Whitefield, both of whom "set perfection so high as to effectively renounce it."[3] For that reason Wesley

141

refused to use the word "absolute" and "perfection" together. There is no such thing as absolute perfection, Wesley argued.

Only God has an "absolute" kind of perfection. All earthly perfection is unfinished. There is an old Japanese saying that every publication should contain a few errors, since to achieve perfection appears conceited and is offensive to the gods. (By the way, I have personally followed this advice slavishly in every one of my books.) Amish quilt makers purposely make mistakes on their masterpieces for the same reason.

The Apache word for "myth" means literally "to tell the holiness."[4] The myth of the Methodist movement is in its telling the holy; its telling the sacred; its telling the holiness. "Telling the holiness" was the theme of Thomas Coke's sermon preached at Barratt's Chapel. In his own diary, Coke told of how in this foundational sermon "I endeavored to set forth our blessed Redeemer, as our Wisdom, Righteousness, Sanctification, and Redemption."[5]

Love has been perfected among us. . . . There is no fear in love, but perfect love casts out fear . . . . Whoever fears has not reached perfection

1 John 4:17, 18

The Methodist "myth" is this simple: if you're going to be a disciple of Jesus, be a disciple that goes *all* the way—from justification to sanctification to glorification. Coke "told the holiness" at Barratt's Chapel. Telling the holiness today is telling people that God has coded their genes and their guts with dreams and abilities that most people never learn to use or explore.

Be all that you can be for God.

Aim for the highest and deepest levels of discipleship.

Don't be satisfied to live only a fraction of the life God has given you.

Don't stop with "good enough." Go for the best. Go for broke. Go the whole way with God.

Dare to let yourself go completely in faith.

Make it your ambition to use your gifts to maximum purpose.

Live the reality of Ephesians 4:13: Don't rest content "until all of us come . . . to maturity, to the measure of the full stature of Christ."

Don't settle for anything but wholeness of mind, body and spirit.

Or as they put it in Wesley's day, aim to be as good a Christian as God can make you.

Christ pleads with us: "I want you just as you are. I'm not calling who you might have been or who you could be. I'm calling you just as you are. I delight in you as you are. I love you. You're all right already for my love. But while I love you just as you are (justification), I don't leave you the way I found you (sanctification). First I call you to 'Get it.' Then I call you to 'Get it right.'"

We do not really know Jesus (the Jesus of the New Testament) if we do not know Him as this poor man, as this (if we may risk the dangerous word) partisan of the poor.

Karl Barth[6]

"Getting it right" is the hermeneutics of holiness—the embodiment of "perfect love" in history and the participation of changed lives in God's mission in the world. The fruit of justification is justice; grace issues in good works. Lived holiness is the synergy of faith and works moving the world from injustice to justice, from cruelty to compassion, from evil to good, from lies to truth. The holiness gene is more than an affair of the heart; justifying and sanctifying grace is an affair of public policy. Spreading scriptural holiness is habitually going about doing good,[7] the "constant, zealous performance of all good works,"[8] the global transformation of the social, economic and political orders so that one can hear God say once again, as God said when the world was created, "it is good."

143

If you aren't going all the way, why go at all?

Joe Namath

In his famous "Love Chapter" Paul told the church at Corinth to aim at "that which is perfect" (*to teleion*), which casts to the side "that which is imperfect" (*ek merous*). Move the soul into a state of spiritual maturity, where the governing rule is not law but love, with faith and hope running close behind. In other words, Paul is calling for the spiritual maturity of "when that which is perfect is come" (1 Corinthians 13:10 KJV). And what is "that which is perfect?" Love. LovePerfect Living!

LovePerfect Living is the essence of what Wesley meant by perfection: "By this everyone will know that you are my disciples, if you love one another" (John 13:35). The perfect Christian is not the one who keeps the commandments, but the one who keeps a right spirit ("right temper" is how Wesley phrased it) and right relationships ("socially responsible" relationships between masters and servants, husbands and wives, church and state, owners and employees); not the one who learns to live by the law, but the one who learns to live by a mind and spirit "which is being renewed in knowledge in the image of its Creator" (Colossians 3:10 NIV).

> This is the sum of Christian perfection: it is all comprised in that one word, love. The first branch of it is the love of God: and as he that loves God loves his brother also.[9]

God does expect perfection. LovePerfect Living is a command: "Be perfect therefore, as your heavenly Father is perfect" (Matthew 5:48). This statement occurs in Jesus' teaching about loving your enemies. In other words, perfection is a relational term that has something to do with eschatology. The word here for "perfect" is *teleios*, a term from Greek aesthetics that means whole, pleasing, something that has integrity. "Be whole even as your Father in heaven is whole" or "Be holy even as your Father in heaven is holy."

The holy energy of LovePerfect Living is a relationship with God and neighbor in which love is the motivating, driving force in a

144

person's personal and social life. LovePerfect living is a right relationship with God and with one another. In John Wesley's famous "Letter to a Roman Catholic" (18 July 1749), he speaks words that deserve immortality: "if we cannot as yet think alike in all things, at least we may love alike."[10]

In fact, if you are living the life of love, or again in Wesley's words, if your faith is "filled with the energy of love,"[11] you are living the perfect life. If love is what motivates you—not rules, not commandments, not outward regulations, but an inward relationship with God and "a habitual disposition of the soul"[12]—then perfection is a reality in your life.

LovePerfect Living is a direction, not a destination.

LovePerfect Living is not immaculate actions, but immaculate aims.

LovePerfect Living is a maturity, integrity, and quality of relationship, not a flawlessness of morality or an ideal of sinlessness.

LovePerfect Living is not walking "in his steps," but walking "in his spirit."

Disease and healing are not just physiological processes. They are spiritual detonations.

Marc Ian Barasch[13]

It was the holiness gene that turned the Wesleyan movement toward the poor so radically that Wesley could say with pride "and surely never in any age or nation, since the Apostles, have those words been so eminently fulfilled, 'the poor have the gospel preached unto them,' as it is at this day."[14] In Wesley's primer for children, one of the first lessons a child learned was not to save money for himself or herself, but to "give all the rest to the Poor."[15]

In fact, scholars such as Theodore Jennings, Donald W. Dayton, and others have found "buried in the Methodist tradition" a significant history of a Wesleyan "preferential option for the poor."[16] Jennings goes so far as to argue that "the criterion of Wesley's own work is the benefit of the poor," that in every aspect of Methodism, "the criterion of the benefit of the poor prevailed," and "solidarity with the poor is . . . the norm of all activity of the people called Methodists."[17] The inward journey of holiness concludes in the outward journey of justice. Or in the words of the twelfth-century monastic writer William of Saint Thierry, the love of truth drives us from the human world to God; the truth of love sends us from God back to the human world.[18]

This genetic commitment to the poor and outcast has placed the Methodist movement on the front lines of social justice ministries. Wesley opposed the slave trade, and in early American Methodism slave-holding was a bar to membership. Only when Methodists lost their identification with the "other" and opted for "respectability" in the eyes of the culture did the church tolerate slave-holding. Pilgrims in the true Wesleyan way led the abolition movement in the nineteenth century, and the civil rights movement in the twentieth century. While the issue of race has been one of the most thorny and fractious thickets in the church, there are historic reasons why African-American churches today tend to be either Methodist or Baptist.

The Methodists were the first people that brought glad tidings to the colored people. I feel thankful that ever I heard a Methodist Preach. We are beholden to the Methodists, under God, for the light of the Gospel we enjoy.

Richard Allen[19]

Methodist hospitality to the social margins led to significant innovations. Methodists went to wherever the poor were to preach: open fields, market places, or public hangings. Even more, Methodists visited the poor on their own turf and strove to establish intimate relationships with them. For Charles Wesley it was not enough to be socially engaged; one had to make the poor and outcast one's "best friends." Wesley's spiritual descendants were champions of economic and social reforms because those "reforms" had faces and names. Francis Place was no friend of the Methodists. But in 1829, looking back on what they had accomplished in England, he confessed: "I am certain I risk nothing when I assert that more good has been done to the people in the last thirty years than in the three preceding centuries."[20]

Methodism's pioneering use of the current technology of the day was not some elitist reverie, but a driving ambition to make the most cutting-edge technology serve the interests of the poor. Hence Methodism's extensive publishing program using tracts, abridgments, libraries.

Other social manifestations of the holiness gene in the eighteenth century were food pantries, homeless shelters, credit unions, job cooperatives and employment agencies. In the 1890s Methodists again got into health care in a typically big way—hospitals, sanitoriums, homes for the aged, and orphanages.

One of the most overlooked evidences of the holiness gene was the historical Wesleyan concern for health. For Wesley, Jesus Christ was "the Medicine of Life" (to quote the fourth-century Syrian theologian Ephrem, one of Wesely's favorite ancient writers).[21] A life of holiness was a prescription for a healthy life.

It was this holiness gene that made Wesley one of the most important names in the history of medicine. Wesley established history's first "people's clinic," a dispensary attached to his chapel, which helped the poor who were sick and couldn't afford a physician. Wesley's historic medical handbook for the common people, *Primitive Physic*, was a compilation of some eight hundred remedies Wesley had tried and found useful in his dispensary.[22]

And He sent them out . . . to heal.

Luke 9:2

With Jesus "The Great Physician" as their model, eighteenth-and nineteenth-century itinerants took their healing role seriously as mini-physicians, indeed the only "physicians" many pioneers regularly saw. An early Methodist itinerant was an eighteenth/nine-

147

teenth-century Marcus Welby for the whole family, including the horse. Many things we take for granted today were used by our ancestors as medicinal treatments. As late as 1929 the soft drink Seven-Up was first marketed as a hangover cure "for home and hospital use."

But physicians with the #3 gene work harder to keep people from getting sick than making sick people well. It is true, of course, that no matter how healthy the body, it's a condemned building. But the Wesleyan doctrine of holiness taught that faith does not so much make sick people well as keep well people well for as long as possible. Holiness keeps people from getting sick.

The #3 gene moves the church from a sickness paradigm to a wellness paradigm; from a sin paradigm to a holiness paradigm; from church growth to church health. The #3 gene forces our churches to "go holistic" and move from being Illness Centers to Total Wellness Centers.

There is a beloved old buzzsaw that displays our defective alleles in sharp relief: "The Church is not a museum for saints, but a hospital for sinners." As mindlessly as we recite this ancient "truism," we are reciting something that is only half-true, and something that puts the wrong half first. It is not in our Wesleyan genes to think of the body of Christ as a mechanism of disease rather than a mechanism of health. Sanctification and holy living stop people from getting sick. The #3 gene keeps cells and communities healthy.

Communities and mechanisms of health look and feel different than communities and mechanisms of disease. The #3 gene builds communities based on hope and holiness and health, not disease and sin and sickness. When churches, and even small groups, become focused on pain and abuse, they can quickly become illness groups rather than recovery groups. William James said a century ago that religion can be debilitating or vitalizing, sick or healthy. Might American religious life be so sick because its paradigm is sickness rather than health?

David Larsen puts it like this: "You can't put live chicks under a dead hen." Joe Aldrich adds his own gloss: "God is not in the business of putting healthy babies in sick incubators."[23]

A cartoon of a pig reads, "Do not try to teach a pig to sing—it wastes your time and it annoys the pig."[24] How many of us are trying to teach pigs to sing all the time in our churches? Rabbi Edwin

Friedman once argued that systems are predisposed to adapt to their weakest members, not to their most creative. Those continually calling the shots are the ones who are the most dependent and the least motivated.[25] Two management consultants, Paula Nelson and Donald Clifton, argue that most organizations live by the motto "Fixing weaknesses will make everything all right." What we do is "fix what's wrong," and let the strengths "take care of themselves." In their book *Soar with Your Strengths* (1992), they argue that we must build upon strengths, rather than mend weaknesses.[26] Perhaps the greatest basketball cliche of our day is, "Remember what got you here." Build on the strengths that got you where you are, not the weaknesses.

Let me illustrate the focused energies of healing another way. What does prayer do? Does prayer keep us healthy and whole, or does prayer heal us? Some say it does the former. Some say it does the latter. The #3 gene says it does both.[27] Wholeness consists of illness and health, light and dark, laughter and tears.[28]

Do not the Gospels move us beyond a "church growth" mentality into a "church health" mentality?[29] The promise of the Gospels is not "growth." The promise is health—a healthy relationship with God, and a healthy lifestyle of wholeness or holiness where spirit, mind and body work and play together. To move from church growth to church health is to move from taking care of people who get sick to stopping people from getting sick. Let's stop getting sick. What if our churches became Wellness Centers on the Information Superhighway? Holiness Stations on the King's Highway?

The medical world is making this shift. In the world of hospital medicine, there is a new movement called "healing health care" which is aimed, not so much to "fix" the part of the patient that is broken and which brought them to the hospital, but is designed to help the whole patient live a healthy life. The whole focus of medicine is now shifting to keeping people well. In Japan the custom is to pay your physician when you're well, and stop paying your physician when you're sick. Recent changes in HMO payments increase the payments to physicians for preventative medicine, and decrease the payments for curative medicine.

Even the law enforcement world is making this shift. In the first six months of 1995, New York City reported a 31 percent decrease in the homicide rate from 1994; as of 1995, NYC ranks twenty-first in

149

overall crime of the twenty-five most populated cities in the U.S., compared with eighteenth in 1993. Why? One reason is that police promotions are now tied, not to the number of arrests they make, but to their ability to keep crime out of their territory. They have stopped measuring crime management and started measuring crime prevention.[30]

Church health means spiritual growth in members less than physical growth in numbers. The issue is not the number who go to Sunday school; but the number who grow in grace and in Bible knowledge. Baptist theologian Darrell W. Robinson, in his wonderful book *Total Church Life*, says that church growth should never be the goal. It is the result of a healthy body of Christ filled with Christ's spirit; or in his words "evangelism is the outflow of the overflow of the Christ-life in a church body."[31] If the Christbody community is judged by the "health" rather than the "growth" standard, then the body may be either shrinking, stable, or swelling. Sometimes a "healthy" body is a body that is losing weight, not staying the same or "growing."

The great Dutch theologian Hendrik Kraemer is alleged to have given an unexpected answer when asked how the churches of Europe were doing at the end of the Second World War. "Oh," he is supposed to have said, "the church is doing much better—attendance is down!"

The story may be too good to be true. But it illustrates the theological and ecclesiological significance of the #3 gene. In the face of a tragic capitulation of so much of the prewar church to Nazism, church growth under Hitler spelled both hypocrisy and heresy.

I know some mega-churches, many struggling for breath while passing the baton from founder to successor or after dropping the baton in sexual immorality and financial irregularity, that are unhealthy to the point where they are dangerous. I know some small rural churches that contain the seeds, fruits and flowers of robust health, and hints of heavens yet unknown—and vice versa.

Where in the Scriptures does Jesus celebrate volume growth over making better use of what we already have to reach higher and deeper dimensions of the divine? Theology must begin with Jesus Christ as encountered in the gospel stories. Jesus is not your model church growth leader. Jesus did not have a church growth ministry. Jesus had a health ministry. Jesus' teachings are a prescribed health regimen. The Sermon on the Mount is a prescription for a healthy lifestyle.

The Wesleyan tradition offers a health spirituality of full-spectrum fitness.

NetNotes

http://www.leonardsweet.com/netboo ks /gateways/

Here you will find links to Joe Namath, Karl Barth, *Primitive Physic* by John Wesley, links to various John Wesley sermons, the Methodist Articles of Religion and other Methodist documents and other Health and Holiness related URLs. Selected images include the healing instruments of Cooper and other Health and Holiness-related images. Your answers and comments about the "Rock-the-Cradle Discussion Questions and Activities" can be posted on the Gateways Forum under the Health & Holiness Listing. The resources listing includes all indexed notes from the chapter, plus you can post additional resources under the Gateways Forum Health & Holiness Listing.

Rock-the-Cradle Discussion Questions and Genogram Exercises

1. Distribute and read Wesley's sermon "On Patience" (1784) where he deals with what the Bible means by this phrase "Ye shall then be perfect." Or distribute and read Wesley's classic sermon, "The Use of Money" (1760) or "The Good Steward" (1768), both of which were precipitated by Wesley's worry that an increasingly rich second generation of Methodists would forget their heritage.[32]

2. Do a Bible study of this text from Matthew 5:43-48. Consult what the commentaries say. Fred Craddock, in his exegesis of Jesus' command to "Be Perfect," notes how the discussion takes place within the context of relationships. To say that we are to be perfect as God is perfect is to say that since God loves completely, fully,

wholly, not partially, so we are to love one another fully, wholly, not partially.[33]

Walter Wink translates this verse "You therefore must be all-inclusive, as your heavenly Abba is all-inclusive."[34] Does this rendition speak to you or not?

3. Ask members of the class to bring in their favorite self-help books. To what extent can these volumes be seen as exercises in perfection? How else does one explain their phenomenal popularity, such that *The New York Times* has had to publish a separate best-seller list for them?

4. In one week's time, see how many book titles, television programs, and other such things members of the group can locate that have the word *perfect* in them.

5. United Methodist Bishop Robert Morgan of the Mississippi Area warns that North American United Methodists have found it easier to build new sanctuaries than build Christian disciples, to study the Bible than to live the Bible, to do social action than to confront people with the challenge of Jesus Christ. How would you respond to his warning?

6. Wesley viewed the visitation of the poor as a key spiritual discipline. "He could no more imagine a week without visiting the hovels of the poor," Theodore W. Jennings, Jr. has written, "than he could a week without participation in the Eucharist."[35] What would visitation of the poor look like today?

7. Even before consumerist culture, Wesley laid down this rule of consumption: "Everything about thee which cost more than Christian duty required thee to lay out is the blood of the poor."[36] Is this an impossibly high standard?

8. To what extent is our church falling under the "Curse of Wesley"?

Lay this deeply to heart, ye who are now a poor, despised, afflicted people. . . . Hitherto ye are not able to relieve your own poor. But if ever your substance increase, see that ye be not straitened in your bowels . . . that ye fall not into the same snare of the devil. Before any of you either lay up treasures on earth, or indulge needless expense of any kind, I pray the Lord God to scatter you to the corners of the earth, and blot out your name from under heaven.[37]

9. Discuss Article 10 ("Of Good Works") and Article 24 ("Of Christian Men's Goods") from *The Articles of Religion of the Methodist Church* (1784), as found in *The Book of Discipline*.

Article 10: "Although good works, which are the fruits of faith, and follow after justification, cannot put away our sins, and endure the severity of God's judgment; yet are they pleasing and acceptable to God in Christ, and spring out of a true and lively faith, insomuch that by them a lively faith may be as evidently known as a tree is discerned by its fruit.

Article 24: "The riches and goods of Christians are not common as touching the right, title, and possession of the same, as some do falsely boast. Notwithstanding, every man ought, of such things as he possesseth, liberally to give alms to the poor, according to his ability."[38]

10. Sing the Charles Wesley stewardship hymn based on Acts 4:34-35. The third stanza goes:

Jesus, thy church inspire
    With Apostolic love,
Infuse the one desire
    T'insure our wealth above:
Freely with earthly goods to part
And joyfully sell all in heart.[39]

11. An excellent resource guide on how the church can help the homeless is called *Rebuilding Our Communities*, and is available from World Vision at 1-800-448-6479.

153

TWO

The MUSIC Gene

Open, Lord, my inward ear,
And bid my heart rejoice;
Bid my quiet spirit hear
Thy comfortable voice;
Never in the whirlwind found
Or where earthquakes rock the place,
Still and silent is the sound,
 The whisper of thy grace.

Charles Wesley[1]

Call it a "still small voice" (1 Kings 19:12 Tyndale, KJV, NKJV, RSV); call it the "sound of thin silence" (John Gray-O.T. Library); call it the "whisper of a gentle breeze" (Ronald Knox); call it the "breath of a light whisper" (Moffatt); call it the "sound of sheer silence" (NRSV); call it a "low murmuring sound" (NEB); call it a "faint murmuring sound" (NJB); call it a "calm, low voice" (New World translation); call it the "sound of gentle stillness" (J. M. Powis Smith); call it the "murmur of a gentle breeze" (Christian Community Bible—Philippines, 1988); call it the "soft whisper of a voice" (GNB); call it the "sound of a soft breath" (Basic English—C.K. Ogden); call it a "tiny whispering sound" (NAB); call it a "still, gentle rustling" (Keil & Delitzsch); call it a "soft murmuring sound" (TANAKH); call it a "gentle little breeze" (Simon J. DeVries—Word Biblical Commentary); call it a "gentle whisper" (NIV).

Call it what you will.

But call it God.

We are living in a culture that is desperately calling for God. To the utter astonishment of rationalists and positivists, spiritual energies and religious impulses have resurfaced on the global scene with tremendous force in recent years. Futurists Faith Popcorn and Lys Marigold argue that "we're at the start of a Great Awakening." We are living, they say, in "a time of spiritual upheaval and religious revival."[2] People are wanting and waiting to invest in spiritual capital. Even scholars who don't make such claims see a need for spiritual awakening. "We can wonder if some kind of a religious revival or religious innovation is not essential even in our own midst," social historian Peter Stearns confesses as he looks at the rot cankering the roots of global urban society.[3]

Postmodern culture is in harmonic clash. The rhythm of our souls is out of harmony with the resonance of God's creation. In the midst of an age of great spiritual yearning, the mainline church, suffering from "lost members, lost young people, lost finances, and, especially, lost self-confidence,"[4] is as much in need of a spiritual awakening as the rest of the culture.

It was into a world of dissonance and dissolution that Methodism launched one of the greatest spiritual awakenings in history. How did they do it? We have explored nine features of the genes and genius of Methodism. But there is more, as we see in the #2 genetic gateway to spiritual awakening out of the Wesleyan tradition.

The Wesleys used the fuel of music to launch Enlightenment souls into the outer and inner spaces of God's presence. Or to use a less anachronistic metaphor, John and Charles Wesley believed that true religion needs music as much as bread pudding needs bread.

In my opinion the two most important languages of humanity, theology and music, have the task of communicating precisely where other forms of communication are no longer possible.

Theologian/activist Dorothee Soelle[5]

155

As the preface to the 1933 *Methodist Hymn Book* put it, "Methodism was born in song." It is true that Methodism "raised hymn singing to a distinctive religious art form."[6] It is also true that Methodism expressed itself as a "sung theology," even a "lyrical religion." John Wesley called his hymnbook of 1780 "a body of experimental and practical divinity." Charles Wesley wrote hymns for every possible incident in life, hymns to help the pilgrim get through every conceivable life experience. No wonder the Wesley brothers produced the greatest outpouring of hymnody in Christian history. After a half-century of evangelical revival, the Wesleys had published sixty-four collections of hymns and three collections of tunes. Wesleyan hymns put creedal affirmations to communal songs; they brought theology to the masses through religious forms of folk poetry and ballads: they are at the same time street simple and university sophisticated. Take this Charles Wesley "hymn" or love poem that will move generations until time stops:

> O Thou who camest from above,
>   The pure celestial fire to impart,
> Kindle a flame of sacred love
>   Upon the mean altar of my heart.
> There let it for thy glory burn
>   With inextinguishable blaze,
> And trembling to its source return,
>   In humble prayer and fervent praise.
> Jesus, confirm my heart's desire
>   To work and speak and think for thee;
> Still let me guard the holy fire,
>   And still stir up thy gift in me.
> Ready for all thy perfect will,
>   My acts of faith and love repeat,
> Till death thy endless mercies seal,
>   And make my sacrifice complete.[7]

But what is most true about the music of the Wesleyan revival is that Methodism constructed a sound theology and a sonic spirituality.[8] The Greek word *cathecesis* is based on our word "echo." The soundness of Wesleyan doctrine, the very soundness of the movement itself, was based on Methodism's coming to terms with sound.

156

The strength of Methodist *cathecesis* was its echoing back to God the "music of the spheres."

For early Methodists, sacred sound was as important as sacred time, sacred space, and sacred image. Like few others in history before him, the Wesley brothers understood what Paul meant when he wrote "nothing is without sound" (1 Corinthians 14:10-11). Methodists turned the society of their day upside down because they knew the meaning of sound, and used sound to help people experience God. They listened souls into existence by hearing into song first Christ and then each other.[9]

Any chance this postmodern culture may have of achieving a new state of harmony depends on our ability to sing it to new life. For Wesleyans, to sing is a sound thing to do.

I

If we are to address the spiritual hungers of our time like our ancestors addressed the spiritual yearnings of their day, we must be cautious about investing so much in vision at the expense of vibration. To be sure, church consultants have decided that only "visionary leadership" will fill up our pews again. In fact, there is so much stress on "vision" that one book even defines "vision" as the "highest calling and truest purpose of leadership."[10] Pastors are rushing whole congregations off to "vision quests" and "visioning retreats" and flocking in packs to conferences that outline how to build "vision teams."

Yet if we trust our genetic inheritance, Wesleyans will go beyond rational and visual approaches to leadership and embrace the sonic dimensions of theology. The "boob tube" may have replaced the "squawk box" as our favorite form of entertainment. A visualholic culture may have made hearing a second-call sense where "seeing" is believing, where you "watch" your back.

But the biblical as well as Wesleyan way forward is not one that "looks" before it leaps. It is, rather, one that "hears" that "your soul shall live" (Isaiah 55:3). Why is hearing so important? Because "faith does come from *HEARING* [*fides et audit*], and *HEARING* through the word of Christ" (Romans 10:17 REB).

One joyful experience followed another, and such a heavenly joy pervaded my whole being, as no pen can describe and no mortal can express.
Evangelical Church founder Jacob Albright[11]

What the Wesleys understood like few others in history is that one does not "see" a vision. One "hears" a vision.[12] The ears, not the eyes, are "the gateway to the soul." The #2 gene shifts our attention from eye to ear, from structure to rhythm, from seeing to hearing, from vision to vibration, from matter to energy. Like only a few other religious movements in history (in the Quaker tradition, "listening" is a technology of creation, sitting an activist posture of movement), Methodism understood that the "ear-gate"—so much more developed and sensitive than the "eye-gate"—acts as the natural conduit of connection between the Creator and creation.

We perceive more of the world with our ears than with our eyes. In fact, as Lorenz Oken pointed out long ago, the eye takes us into the world, but the ear takes the world into us. When the eyes take us into the world, they trick us into seeing things that aren't there. That's why God gave us eyelids but not earlids. The eyes are deceitful, easily subject to optical illusions.

We begin life hearing and we end life hearing. Our ears were opened before birth; hearing is the last of the senses to leave us at death. To hear is to be.

When hearing is good, speaking is good.
ancient Egyptian proverb

Our sense of hearing is much more sophisticated and differentiated than our sense of seeing.[13] There are more than three times the number of nerve connections between the ear and the brain than between the eye and the brain. Our eardrum registers smaller impulses than any other sense organ. In fact, the amplitude of the vibrations of our eardrum is around ten to the minus ninth power. That is said to be smaller than the wave length of visible light and even less than the diameter of a hydrogen atom. Given this sensitivity one can understand how the composer Felix Mendelssohn could express frustration that "a piece of music that I love expresses thoughts to me that are not too *imprecise* to be framed in words, but too *precise*. So I find that attempts to express such thoughts in words may have some point to them, but they are also unsatisfying."[14]

Furthermore, our ears can judge and balance as well as measure. The most precise and mathematical sense organ in the body is the ear. Our range of hearing is ten times wider than our range of seeing. You can't *see* that a color emits a light frequency twice that of another one; but you can hear whether a higher tone really swings with a frequency twice that of the lower one.[15] Your ears can hear numbers. Your ears can translate these mathematical numbers into sense perceptions, the material into spiritual. Hans Kayser points out the astonishing fact that our ears are the only human sense organ that is able to perceive numerical *quantity* as well as numerical *value*.[16]

II

It is only now with quantum physics and superstring theory that we are beginning to understand scientifically what the Wesleyan movement intuited right from the start—there is more to life than what meets the eye. When we experience ourselves as music more than matter, when we experience life more as spirit than as substance, all things are possible.

In the quantum world, as in the spirit world, literally anything can happen. Time flows backward as well as forward; linear time and space give way to curved time and space; objects can be created out of nothing; a causal universe becomes an ever-curving universe.

We live in a world that is more weird than we ever imagined—a world that is fractal, self-replicating, inflationary, unpredictable. Just how weird is evidenced in the way mind, matter, and time are part of the same reality. In the quantum world, what appears solid is empty, and what appears empty is full. For example, the energy in one cubic centimeter of empty space is more than the total energy of all the matter in the known universe. The energy in one cubic centimeter of empty space is the equivalent of one trillion atomic bombs.[17]

The German theologian Hans Küng poses the postmodern condition in the following exchange. In the modern era, if you asked a scientist "Do you believe in spirit?" the scientist would respond: "Of course not, I'm a scientist." In the postmodern era, if you ask a scientist "Do you believe in spirit?" the scientist says, "Of course, I'm a scientist."

If you ask me tomorrow or any other day why some sounds are sad and others glad, I shall not be able to tell you. Not even your Papa could tell you that. Why, what a thing to ask, my pets! If you knew that, you would know everything. Good night, my dears, good night.

Rebecca West[18]

Science now believes in an unseen, invisible world. As if to mock modernity's easy opposition of science and theology, postmodern science is reaching conclusions about the universe similar to those reached by religious traditions. The emergence of a new scientific paradigm has led to severe changes of perspective. For example, contemporary physics has found the existence of a parallel world that is accessible only through the lens of symbols and trust. Or to put it in theological terms, contemporary physics has found the existence of a spirit world that is accessible only through the eyes of faith and love.

Scientists are finding that they are no different from theologians—they can only define the universe by taking leaps of faith. The fundamental principle of quantum physics is this: First you believe, then you see. What was it Augustine wrote? "I believe that I might understand." There are things going on in the world that lie beyond common sense, beyond the senses, beyond the ability of the human mind to grasp. Like theologians, scientists increasingly "look not at what can be seen, but at what cannot be seen; for what can be seen is teporary; but what cannot be seen is eternal" (2 Corinthians 4:18). Like theologians, scientists less and less concern themselves with what goes on in what others call "the real world," and more and more concern themselves with what goes on in "the unreal world."[19]

It used to be physicists thought of reality as solid. Matter was real, and mass was a fundamental concept in the world of physics. Now matter has dematerialized. Superstring theory tells us that mass is but one positive form of energy. Mass isn't a "solid object" or "inanimate substance." Matter isn't really matter. Matter and energy are convertible. Matter is movement. Matter is rhythm. Matter is really vibrating threads of energy. Matter is the dance of energy.

If one could totally convert the amount of energy in 1g (0.04 oz) of matter, it would be able to:

- Lift fifteen million people to the top of Mount Everest.
- Boil four liters (a gallon) of water for each of fifty-five million people.
- Supply a modern city of 15,000 people with electricity for a year.[20]

Everything is energy, from heat (released by reactions) to light (emitted by atoms in excited states) to chemistry (the strength of chemical bonds). The universe is comprised of energy. The cosmos is spirit.

As biological beings, basically you and I are "dancing energy." I *think* I am made of matter—and you and I do look solid. But looks are deceiving (remember those eyelids?). When one pushes behind appearances and uncovers the atomic structure of matter, one finds that what appears to be material is nothing more than packets of energy vibrating at different frequencies. And everything that vibrates emits sound.

A stone is frozen music.
Greek philosopher/mathematician Pythagoras

161

The physical foundation of the universe is not made of matter, or substance, but energy fields, non-material presences and relationships. That is why the whole modern concept of "matter" is now discredited and discarded. What we think of as "matter" is really instant manifestations of dense energy fields that surface and then disappear. Matter exists only as a wave of possibility until we try to observe it and gather information about it. At that moment the wave of probability collapses into a particle called an electron.

Chemistry is dancing clouds of electrons that sometimes morph into particles, sometimes meander like waves. No wonder Nobel prize-winning chemist Ilya Prigogine calls this the biggest philosophical crisis since Aristotle's quantitative description of nature. My own educational pilgrimage is the story of the emergence of this postmodern philosophical crisis.

When I went to elementary school, my teachers told me that the smallest piece of matter was an atom. Matter is made up of molecules, and molecules are made up of atoms, each one of which is a solar system in miniature.

When I went to junior high school, my teachers told me that—oops!—an atom was basically empty space with something smaller inside it—a particle called a nucleus.

When I went to high school, my teachers told me that—oops!—a nucleus was basically empty space with something smaller inside it—particles called protons and neutrons.

When I went to college, my physics professor told me that—oops!—protons and neutrons were basically empty space with something smaller inside them—particles called quarks and gluons—the smallest building blocks of matter.

When I began reading physics texts on my own, I learned that—oops!—quarks were basically empty space with something smaller inside them called a "particle zoo": first three quarks, then six quarks: up, down, strange, charm, bottom (beauty), top (truth). The top quark, I learned, is the last elusive piece of matter.

But as the turn of the millennium approaches, Steve Geer of Chicago's Fermilab says that—oops!—the top quark itself may be composed of still smaller pieces of unnamed matter that are so small they have no position in time and space.

III

We live in an ocean of energy. Life is energy. God is pure creative energy. "God is spirit," the life energy of the cosmos. You and I are the emergent human form of organized energy, the mattering of God's spirit.

Music does more than help us experience God as spirit as we experience life as spirit. Music is more accurately the essence of who we are as beings created in the image of God. If the most elemental and elementary aspect of life is energy that vibrates, then life is at base music. For anything that vibrates gives off sound. Sound is a function of vibration, of resonance.

Scuba divers used to talk about the silence of the deep. Astronauts used to talk about the stillness of space. Now we know just how mistaken they were. Everything that is has sound and rhythm—from whales and octopi to supernovas and quasars. Cosmic vibrations are everywhere.[21] From our cells to our cellular phones, from snowflakes to supernovas, everything emits vibrations, sounds to feed or famish the soul.[22]

Celebrate th' eternal God
with harp and psaltery,
timbrels soft and cymbals loud
in this high praise agree;
praise with every tuneful string;
all the reach of heavenly art,
all the powers of music bring,
the music of the heart.

Charles Wesley[23]

You and I are at base *sound*—a human organization of dancing energy. You and I are at base a song. There is not an atom in our body that isn't singing a song. The vibrations and resonances that go on at the atomic level reveal that our entire body was created to *hear-burst into song.* Our beings are bathed in vibrations that unconsciously set the tone and tune of our lives.

Not only does all of creation around us hum with the sounds of life. Our genes, our ganglia, your liver, my lipids, every one of our trillions of cells vibrate. The laws of resonance apply. Anything that vibrates sympathetically responds to vibrations, even the most infinitesimal vibrations we have yet to measure.[24] What are brain waves? Do you see vibrations? Why have soldiers throughout history broken step before crossing a bridge? What do you think brought down the walls of Jericho? Why did Caruso have to watch it when he sang certain notes? One word: vibrations.

Because of vibrations it is more than a metaphor to say that every atom sings a song. Yes, from the standpoint of physics the very nuclei of all atoms make music. But it's even more beautiful and mysterious than that. The cosmos is more than vibrations. From the innumerable vibrations the cosmos could choose, it chooses those vibrations that make "harmonic sense" and ultimately "musical sense." There are more fifty-note melodies to be generated from the eighty-eight keys of a piano keyboard than there are atoms in the entire universe. But each one of these melodies makes beautiful music except when disease and death are present.

The earth sings MI, FA, MI so that you may infer even from the syllables that in this our domicile MIsery and FAmine obtain.

Johann Kepler[25]

The electron shell of the carbon atom, for example, follows the laws of harmonics, producing the tone scale C-D-E-F-G-A. Philosopher/German jazz musician Joachim-Ernst Berendt was the first to observe that this is the hexachord of Gregorian chant. Could it be that all carbon-based life is actually built on the Gregorian chant? Could it be that music makes us before we make music? Could it be that *Mr. Holland's Opus* was right: "Look around you. We are the notes and the melody of your opus. We are the music of your life."

Could it be that disease occurs when the vibrations of a part are out of harmony with the whole, with oneself, with others, with God?

164

Could Novalis be right in naming every disease a musical problem? Could healing and hearing really go together? The Latin word *cantare*, from which we get our word "to sing," meant originally "to work magic," to "heal." *Cantor* was someone who worked magic with music, who worked healing playing sounds. A *cantata* was a healing piece of music.

Creation does more than sound. Creation sings. Composer/conductor Leonard Bernstein lectured constantly from his podium that Genesis 1 is mistranslated "And God said, Let there be light." What brought light and all things into being is best translated "And God sang." Creation was more than a speech event. The Master Musician created the world from sound (cf. Psalm 29). Creation was a musical composition. And creation sings back its praises to God with every vibration of its being.

There is no one who isn't musical. When the constellations of atoms between two people move toward one another—in all their juxtapositions and oppositions—some kind of music is composed. Sometimes the composition is beautiful. People feel they are "in tune with each other"; "on the same wavelength"; "harmonious"; they "make beautiful music together." Other times people feel disharmony: "bad vibes," "personality clashes," and so forth. Resonance reduces entropy in the world. Resonance with God, with one another, and with the physical world diminishes the randomness that engulfs us. Resonance structures physical reality in healing, holistic, "soulistic" ways.

This World is not a Conclusion.
A Species stands beyond—
Invisible, as music—
But Positive, as Sound.[26]

Emily Dickinson

What accompanied the ark as it was brought to Jerusalem? Sound (2 Samuel 6:15). Why, in so many cultures, observes British scholar J. S. Eades, "[are] musical experience and religious experience seen as

165

closely related," and "religion has nearly always involved music in ritual as one of the main means of heightening religious awareness."[27] Why were so many of the church fathers trained in music?

Wesley's organizational genius was to harness the energies of the Spirit and bring the gospel to an emerging Industrial Age accompanied by sound. Wesley gave musical structure to the divine energies of grace. He explored musically the spiritual and social implications of Pentecost for the age in which he lived. He composed a spiritual awakening from the inside out.

It is time descendants of the Wesley brothers live out of our #2 gene. It is in our genes to help postmodern culture understand that being musical doesn't have as much to do with playing an instrument or singing in tune as to a way of living, a hospitality and sensitivity to the Spirit. Name a group better prepared to help postmodern culture read between the lines, hear between the words, sing in parts, strike a resonant chord? For when disciples of Jesus live a musical life, our ears become temples, altars for the presence and power of the living God.[28]

The Gospel of John begins famously: "In the beginning was the *Logos*." But "Logos" means both "Sound" and "Word." Jesus is the Word of God, the Word that which must be heard. Jesus is the Sound of God, The Song Made Flesh.

Jesus as Sound is our tuning fork to the Creator, the Eternal. If we would seek to get our own lives back in tune with God it must be through eliminating outside static and tuning our spirits to the frequencies of God's Spirit, matching the resonance of our actions and attitudes to Jesus' pitch. My personal definition of Jesus is "God's perfect pitch."

Think about it as we close this chapter. Instruments are tuned to 440 cps (cycles per second) for perfect pitch. One can tune instruments looser than that and achieve "relative pitch." But a "relative pitch" instrument sounds good only by itself. When played with other instruments, relative pitch causes dissonance. We may sound okay to ourselves, but when we play alongside others we are not in tune and discover just how out-of-tune we really are.[29]

Postmodern Wesleyans must help people pitch their lives to the perfect pitch of Christ. It is in our genes to assist postmodern culture in seeing moral guides such as the Ten Commandments and the

Beatitudes not as laws, but as musical notes that must be played properly if there is to be harmony in the world and in one's life.

NetNotes

http://www.leonardsweet.com/netbooks/gateways/

This NetNotes has links to hymns from THE Methodist Hymn Book, Life in the Universe with Steven Hawking, Gregorian chants, Emily Dickinson, and various music related URLs. The Interactive page contains the "Gateways Jukebox." Listen to midi files as you experience this chapter of the book. Selected images include the hymn books from Barratt's Chapel and other assorted images. Your answers and comments about the "Rock-the-Cradle Discussion Questions and Genogram Exercises" can be posted on the Gateways Forum under the Music Listing. The resources listing includes all indexed notes from the chapter, plus you can post additional resources under the Gateways Forum Music Listing.

Rock-the-Cradle Discussion Questions and Genogram Exercises

1. Try this experiment. Give someone five seconds to solve this math problem: $8 \times 7 \times 6 \times 5 \times 4 \times 3 \times 2 \times 1 = $_____. Then give someone else five seconds to solve this one: $1 \times 2 \times 3 \times 4 \times 5 \times 6 \times 7 \times 8 = $_____. I will guarantee you that the guesses will be different. On test samples of people, the average answer guessed for the first equation was 2250. The average answer for the second was 512. (Of course, the right answer is 40,320.)

   Why was the guess for the first four times higher than the guess for the second? First impressions mean everything. It all depends on where you start. Where you finish is dependent on where you begin. If something doesn't have a "right spirit" from the beginning, it's going to have a "bad spirit" at the end.

   Spirit comes first!

What kind of spirit do you give off? What is your best spiritual feature? Your worst?

2. Willie Ruff and John Rodgers of Yale University put into a synthesizer the "songs of the planets." They even made a record of it. The six visible planets with their elliptical orbits constitute in Kepler's phrase a "six-part harmony motet," while the outer three planets add the "rhythm section" in which Pluto beats the bass drum.

   Listen to their album *The Harmony of the World*. Or share reactions to David Deamer's *DNA Music*, a musical translation of DNA sequences.[30]

3. Pass out copies of "A Letter to a Young Musician," written by James A. Rogers, Diaconal Minister of Music for over twenty years at First United Methodist Church, Springfield, Illinois, as first published in *Worship Arts*, September–October 1996, 3-5.

4. Discuss the implications of Mary Catherine Bateson's thesis that one shouldn't so much "plan" a life from the outside in as one "composes" a life from the inside out.[31]

5. There is a notion that all art aspires toward the condition of music. Would you agree or disagree?

6. "I heard the Queen Mary blow one midnight . . . and the sound carried the whole history of departure and longing and loss." E. B. White speaks here of sounds that echo a lifetime of thoughts and experiences. What are some of these sounds for your people? Put together some focus groups and find out.

7. Carlyle Marney liked to tell people who complained of God's silence to live on the basis of the last clear word from God they heard until they could hear another one. What was the last clear word from God you have heard?

8. The book *Elevator Music* calls Muzak "furniture music." The thesis of the book is that music is now more than just background; it's become a utilitarian fixture and feature of our environment.[32] Could this be why people are already trying to trademark sounds? Already there are three trademarked sounds: (1) the NBC chimes; (2) the MGM lion, and (3) the Harley-Davidson engine sound of its "Hog"—patent pending. If you could trademark the sound of your church, what would it be?

9. Bach and Handel went blind; Beethoven went deaf. Which do you think would be worse: blindness or deafness?

10. Sing and discuss hymns that teach sound theology, like this one:

This is My Father's world,
and to my listening ears
all nature sings, and round me rings
the music of the spheres.[33]

For more such hymns see
"There's Within My Heart a Melody" (# 380)[34]
"The Voice of God Is Calling" (# 436)
"Take My Life, and Let It Be" (# 399)
"There's a Church Within Us, O Lord"
"Rescue the Perishing" (v. 3) (# 591)
"Come, Thou Fount of Every Blessing" (#400)
"When in Our Music God Is Glorified" (# 68)

ONE

The ALTARS-GATE Gene

The eleven genetic gateways of the Wesleyan tradition may be more important for Century XXI than for Centuries XVIII, XIX, and XX. Or to put it another way, God may have raised up the Wesleyan movement more for the postmodern era than for the modern world.

But it will all come to naught without the #1 gene: Prayer. The Wesleyan Revival was born on its knees.

Prayer is the most powerful force in the universe. But don't believe me. The results of scientific research into the medical benefits of prayer are so overpowering that physicians who don't integrate prayer into their treatments appear almost liable to malpractice suits. As of 1998, there were eleven medical schools in the U.S. that offered specific courses on "prayer and healing" (I am afraid to tally a comparison with divinity schools).

An awakening does not awaken itself; an awakening is awakened—by vigilance, fasting, and prayer. Everyone is asking, "if the fields are ripe, what is wrong with the harvest?" What is wrong is the absence of prayer. Wesley's soul in the morning, noon, and night did pray. Therefore the Sweet family was going to do the same. We gathered first thing in the morning for prayer, we concluded each day with family prayer, and at one point my two brothers and father came home for lunch to pray. I myself was harvested by back-beating Wesleyans who knelt down with me at the camp-meeting altar and beat faith into my backbone as they prayed. It was the spiritual power of Altars-Gate[1] that made Wesley live among my family as a contemporary.

170

When God extends great mercy for his people, the best thing God does is set them a-praying.

Matthew Henry

But don't believe me. Listen to some others in one of the most extraordinary exchanges about the Wesleyan movement to take place in the last century.

Roger Starr is a Jewish liberal Democrat (this is important to the story) who writes widely on issues of housing and the urban crisis for the *New York Times*. He is associated with the New School for Social Research, and teaches at City College of the City University of New York. He also sits on the board of the journal *The Public Interest,* which published a series of articles, one by the executive editor Joel Schwartz, based on some of his arguments comparing twentieth-century New York City and eighteenth-century London.

Both eras were beset by immense problems of drugs (crack today, gin back then, as captured by Hogarth's *Gin Lane*), family disintegration, social disorder, violence. In the England of Wesley's day thousands were left to fend for themselves in harrowing conditions, creating a dependent, self-destructive "underclass."

"The streets were dark with something more than night" perfectly catches the feel of eighteenth-century London as well as twentieth-century New York. The streets of London were blanketed with fear and stalked by "footpads" and "highwaymen" (today we call them "carjackers" and "criminals"). Yet what saved London was a social leader named John Wesley, who addressed the "demoralization" of his day with a "remoralization" message that empowered the poor to lead their own crusade in fighting social injustice, economic exploitation and spiritual impoverishment.

George Will is a serious-minded, bow-tied Roman Catholic conservative Republican (this is important to the story) who writes political commentary for *Newsweek* and *The Washington Post*. After studying the suggestion from Starr and others, he wrote a syndicated column agreeing with the thesis of the importance of this social movement known as "The Wesleyan Awakening." He confessed that it was hard to swallow agreement with such liberal types as Starr, but admitted that not everything liberals say is wrong.

In his own research, Will discovered that the England of Wesley's day—then the most powerful nation on the face of the earth—suffered many problems similar to those which plague the U. S. today. Drug addictions were rife—most notoriously gin-makers and gin-heads then, crack-houses and crack-heads today. Youth gangs were terrorizing the cities. Much of England's population languished in squalor and worked in dehumanizing smokestack factories. The church and its clergy had forgotten the poor and the working classes, and had opted for an establishment respectability.

Wesley changed all this. His societies became distribution centers for food, clothing, money and medicine for the poor. They also became lending banks, housing finders, job training centers and legal aid and advice drop-ins. Wesley started history's first people's medical clinic, and he led the social struggles of his day for prison reform and abolition of slavery. Wesley put it like this: "The Gospel of Christ knows of no religion but social; no holiness, but social holiness. . . . This commandment have we from CHRIST, that he who loves God loves his brother also."[2]

Amazingly, Will ends the first paragraph of his column with these words: "New York, like many other cities, needs a man on horseback. . . . It needs John Wesley." The only thing that will save our cities, Will writes, is a "cohort of contemporary Wesleys." And he ends his article with: "Does anyone have a better idea?"[3]

This amazing exchange caught the eye of Fred Barnes, the editor of *The New Republic* and an evangelical Episcopalian moderate (this is important to the story). In a "Washington Diary" column, Barnes deemed Will and Starr strange bedfellows but worthy boarders. Barnes registered both agreement and disagreement with both of them. Barnes agreed that the world today needs another Wesley, but found Will's and Starr's analysis coming up short.

Both of them forgot one thing: "the source of Wesley's power was religious faith, and religion of a peculiarly social kind. Wesley's evangelism was inseparable from his social activism." People today are not just hungry for the things of the world, but for the things of the spirit. "A secular Wesley with tips on how to shake poverty won't grip the underclass. A religious Wesley, a new Martin Luther King, Jr., might. I understand why Will didn't play up Wesley's religious appeal. Some people insist that religion not only can't solve social problems, it shouldn't even enter the national debate on them at all. I disagree on both counts."[4]

Only God's solutions are as big as the problems. Only God's answers are as big as the questions.

My very favorite Wesley story takes place over a century after Wesley dies. An elderly African gentleman visited King's Road Chapel, where Wesley is buried, and asked the minister-in-charge if he might visit Wesley's grave. The priest accompanied the man to the grave where the man stood in silence for a moment. He then asked "Might a body pray here?" The minister replied "Feel free."

The man knelt and with one hand on Wesley's grave and other uplifted to the heavens, he prayed: "Lord . . . Do it again! Lord . . . Do it again."

Lord . . . Do it again!

NetNotes

http://www.leonardsweet.com/netbooks/gateways/

Here you will find links to prayer groups from around the world, including Internet Prayer Pages, the NCCUMC Prayer Page and other selective URLs. The interactive page contains the "Gateways Prayer Page." It is a place to post your own prayer concerns and share with others. Selected images include the altar rail and the Asbury/Coke Star at Barratt's Chapel and prayer-related images. Listen to a midi of "Sweet Hour of Prayer" in the Gateways Jukebox as you experience this chapter of the book. Your answers and comments about the "Rock-the-Cradle Discussion Questions and Activities" can be posted on the Gateways Forum under the Prayer Listing. The resources listing includes all indexed notes from the chapter, plus you can post additional resources under the Gateways Forum Prayer Listing.

Rock-the-Cradle Discussion Questions and Genogram Exercises

1. Conduct a churchwide "Concert of Prayers," as outlined in Leonard I. Sweet and Karen Elizabeth Rennie, "Concert of Prayers," *Homiletics*, January–March 1996, 11-14.

NOTES

Acknowledgments

1. *Gates of Excellence* (New York: E.P. Dutton, 1988), 63.

Introduction

1. Peter Gabriel, "Biko," ©1980, Charisma Records, in *Peter Gabriel [3]*, UNI/Geffen, released 07/07/87.

2. Leonard I. Sweet Sr., *Chartnotes: Sailing New Seas* (Dayton: Whaleprints, 1995).

3. "Firing Line: Q and A," Interview with *Technotrends* author Daniel Burrus, *Performance* (September 1995), 16.

4. Matthew Arnold, "The Grand Chartreuse," *Essays and Poems of Arnold*, with an introduction by Frederick William Roe (New York: Harcourt, Brace, 1934), 446.

5. Philip Gross, "Mugshot," in his *I.D.* (London: Faber and Faber, 1994), 35.

6. Gabriel García Márquez, *One Hundred Years of Solitude* (New York: Harper & Row, 1970), 1.

7. Dannie Abse, *Ask the Bloody Horse* (London: Hutchinson, 1986), 5.

8. Darrell Jodock, *The Church's Bible: Its Contemporary Authority* (Minneapolis: Fortress, 1989), 87.

9. Fay Weldon, *Wicked Women: A Collection of Short Stories* (London: Flamingo, 1995); as reviewed in Alev Adil, "Cunning Sirens," *Times Literary Supplement*, 8 December 1995, 19. The Presbytery of Greater Atlanta recently (1996) had to decide whether a transsexual could retain the ordination conferred on her when she was a man. They decided 186 to 161 that she could.

10. Vaclav Havel, "A Time for Transcendence," *Utne Reader* (January–February 1995), 53.

11. Ibid.

12. Dennis N. Paulson, "The Demise of The United Methodist Church," *Michigan Christian Advocate*, 29 January 1996, 1.

13. Quoted in G. B. May, "Guitry's One-Man Band," *Times Literary Supplement*, 7 October 1994, 13.

14. Colin Morris, *Wrestling with an Angel* (London: Collins Fount, 1990), 28.

15. Roger Finke and Rodney Stark, *The Churching of America, 1776-1990: Winners and Losers in Our Religious Economy* (New Brunswick: Rutgers University Press, 1992).

16. For the reproduction crisis of the mainline church, see my essay "The Ladder and the Cross: The Plover Report," *Bibelot* 3:1 (1988), eight-page insert.

17. The United Methodist Church. General Council on Ministries. Office of Research, *A Profile of United Methodists Based on the Survey of United Methodist*

Opinion: A Research Project to Provide Information for Informed Decision-making (Dayton: The Council on Ministries, 1995), 5.

18. David A. Roozen, William McKinney, and Wayne Thompson, "The 'Big Chill' Generation Warms to Worship: A Research Note," *Review of Religious Research* 31 (March 1990), 314-22.

19. Robert Minhinnick, *The Looters* (Bridgend: Seren Books, 1989), 19-20.

20. Lyle E. Schaller, "Foreword" to Richard P. Schowalter, *Igniting a New Generation of Believers* (Nashville: Abingdon, 1995), 7.

21. Herb Miller, "Demythologizing the Baby Buster Challenge," *Net Results* 16 (November 1995), 6. See also Penny Long Marler, "Lost in the Fifties: The Changing Family and the Nostalgic Church," in Wade Clark Roof and Nancy Ammerman, eds., *Work, Family and Religion in Contemporary Society* (New York: Routledge, 1995), 23-60.

22. "Calling All Cars," *The Boomer Report* (December 1995), 5.

23. John Naisbitt and Patricia Aburdene, *Megatrends 2000: Ten New Directions for the 1990's* (New York: William Morrow, 1990), 270-97, laud "religious revival" as one of the megatrends of the 90s.

24. Ronald Inglehart, "Changing Religious Organizations, Gender Rolls, and Sexual Norms," chapter 6 of *Culture Shift in Advanced Industrial Society* (Princeton: Princeton University Press, 1990), 177-211. The quote is from 187.

25. Genetech (San Francisco) became the first company established to commercialize rDNA technology.

26. Jeff Lyon and Peter Gorner, *Altered Fates: Gene Therapy and the Retooling of Human Life* (New York: Norton, 1995), 532.

27. Philip Kitcher, *The Lives to Come: The Genetic Revolution and Human Possibilities* (New York: Simon & Schuster, 1996), 40.

28. The recipe book analogy comes from Francis Crick. The latter analogy comes from Lyon and Gorner, *Altered Fates*, 531.

29. These figures were developed by Lawrence M. Krauss, *The Physics of Star Trek* (New York: Basic Books, 1995), 76-77. To clarify this concept he adds: "The storage requirements for a human pattern are ten thousand times as large compared to the information in all the books ever written, as the information in all the books ever written is compared to the information of this page" (77).

30. See Greg Blonder, "Faded Genes," *Wired* (March 1995), 107.

31. Chet Raymo, "Of Dragons and Hypogriffs," in *The Virgin and the Mousetrap: Essays in Search of the Soul of Science* (New York: Viking, 1991), 167.

32. Kitcher, *The Lives to Come*, 268.

33. See Sharon Begley, "Holes in Those Genes," *Newsweek*, 15 January 1996, 57.

34. Of these 2,800 companies, 20 percent are oil, chemical, drug, food, and agribusiness corporations like Bayer, Ciba-Geigy, Coca Cola, Amatil, Dupont, Exxon, Hoechst, ICI, Limagrain, Monsanto, Pioneer Hi-Bred, Rhone-Poulenc, Sandoz, Unilever, and others.

35. *John Naisbitt's Trend Letter*, 14 (3 August 1995), 4.

36. For an elaboration of this concept, see Murray Gell-Mann, *The Quark and the Jaguar: Adventures in the Simple and the Complex* (New York: Freeman, 1994).

37. The best introduction to the nature and function of genetic engineering from a Christian perspective is Ronald Cole-Turner, *The New Genesis: Theology and the Genetic Revolution* (Louisville: Westminster/John Knox Press, 1993).

38. T. S. Eliot, *T. S. Eliot: Collected Poems, 1909-1962.* (New York: Harcourt, Brace & World, 1962), 182, 207-208.

39. "Minutes of Several Conversations Between the Rev. Mr. Wesley and Others from the Year 1744 to the Year 1789," in *The Works of Reverend John Wesley, A.M.* (New York: B. Blaugh and T. Mason, 1835), 5:235.

40. John Wesley, to "Our Brethren in America," 10 September 1784, in *The Letters of the Rev. John Wesley, A.M.*, ed. John Telford (London: Epworth, 1931), 7:238-39.

41. For example, originally everyone entered Barratt's Chapel through the ground floor. The doors on the west wall were at first windows. They were changed to doors in the years immediately before the Civil War because the members of the increasingly middle-class congregation objected to having to mingle with the Black worshipers coming down out of the balcony. Historian Allen Clark suspects that the reason why all four of the Black Methodist churches organized in the area during the mid-nineteenth century opted for the AME rather than the ME affiliation was because of the increasingly frigid reception given Black worshipers at Barrett's Chapel.

42. M. Douglas Meeks, ed., *What Should Methodists Teach? Wesleyan Tradition and Modern Diversity* (Nashville: Kingswood, 1990), 139.

43. John Wesley, "Thoughts upon Methodism" (1786) in *The Methodist Societies: History, Nature, and Design*, ed. Rupert E. Davies, *The Works of John Wesley* (Nashville: Abingdon, 1989), 9:527.

44. Theodore Roszak, "Living Dread," *21-C* (Jume 1996), 65.

45. Robyn Williams, "Science Function," *21-C* (April 1995), 88.

46. Egbert Schuurman, *Perspectives on Technology and Culture* (Sioux Center: Dordt College Press, 1995), 122.

Chapter 11: The TIMING Gene

1. Charles Wesley, second stanza, "A Charge to Keep I Have," *The United Methodist Hymnal: Book of United Methodist Worship* (Nashville: The United Methodist Publishing House, 1989), 413.

2. See Leonard I. Sweet, *FaithQuakes* (Nashville: Abingdon, 1994).

3. *The Gospel According to Thomas*, trans. A. Guillaumont, H.-Ch. Puech, G. Quispel, W. Till and Yassah 'Abd al Masih (Leiden: Brill, 1959), Log. 91.

4. *Book of Discipline of The United Methodist Church*, ¶321.17.a (Nashville: The United Methodist Publishing House, 1996), 227.

5. Robert DeMaria Jr., *Samuel Johnson and the Life of Reading* (Baltimore: Johns Hopkins University Press, 1997), 217.

6. William M. Easum, *Sacred Cows Make Gourmet Burgers: Ministry Anytime, Anywhere, by Anybody* (Nashville: Abingdon, 1995), 125.

7. Ibid., 126.

8. John Maxwell, *The Winning Attitude: Your Key to Personal Success* (Nashville: Thomas Nelson, 1993), 94.

9. John Wesley to Mrs. Johnson, 26 September 1784, *The Letters of John Wesley*, ed. John Telford (London: Epworth, 1931), 7:241.

10. Kevin Phillips, *Arrogant Capital: Washington, Wall Street, and the Frustration of American Politics* (Boston: Little, Brown, 1994), 165.

11. John Wesley, "Satan's Devices," *Sermons*, ed. Albert C. Outler, in *The Works of John Wesley* (Nashville: Abingdon, 1985), 2:148.

12. Phillips, *Arrogant Capital*, 167-68.

13. Hillel Schwartz, *Century's End: An Orientation Manual Toward the Year 2000*, rev. and abridged ed. (New York: Doubleday Currency, 1996), 155.

14. For a similar analogy that parallels late-nineteenthth and late-twentiethth century feminisms, see Elaine Showalter, *Sexual Anarchy: Gender and Culture at the Fin de Siecle* (New York: Viking, 1990).

15. Russell E. Richey, Kenneth E. Rowe, Jean Miller Schmidt, *The Methodist Experience in America* (Nashville: Abingdon, forthcoming).

16. Nathan O. Hatch, *The Democratization of American Christianity* (New Haven: Yale University Press, 1989).

17. Aleksandr Kushner, "We Don't Get to Change Our Century," in *Apollo in the Snow: Selected Poems*, trans. Paul Graves and Carol Ueland (New York: Farrar, Straus and Giroux, 1991), 36-37.

18. See Hatch, *The Democratization of American Christianity*.

19. Evan Esar, *Esar's Comic Dictionary* (Garden City, N.Y.: Doubleday, 1983), 244.

20. Harry Emerson Fosdick, "God of Grace and God of Glory," *The United Methodist Hymnal*, 577.

21. Thanks to Donald J. Shelby, "It's Hard to Be a Christian When It's Easy," sermon preached 23 May 1993, Santa Monica (California) United Methodist Church.

Chapter 10: The FAST LEARNING/UNLERNING Gene

1. Charles Wesley, "At the Opening of a School at Kingswood," *Representative Verse of Charles Wesley*, ed. Frank Baker (London: Epworth, 1962), 143.

2. For the centrality of spirituality to education, see James Moffett, *The Universal Schoolhouse: Spiritual Awakening Through Education* (San Francisco: Jossey-Bass, 1994), esp. 3-32.

3. For a more extensive exploration of these three dimensions, see my *Quantum Spirituality: A Postmodern Apologetic* (Dayton: Whaleprints, 1991).

4. Thomas Coke, *Extracts of the Journals of the Rev. Coke's Five Visits to America* (London: G. Paramore, 1793), 16.

5. See Easum, *Sacred Cows Make Gourmet Burgers*, where he laments: "Making decisions and controlling what happens is more important . . . than making disciples" (11).

6. Leander E. Keck, *The Church Confident* (Nashville: Abingdon, 1993), 45.

7. William J. Reynolds, *Companion to Baptist Hymnal* (Nashville: Broadman, 1976), 20.

8. Knute Larson, *Growing Adults on Sunday Morning* (Wheaton: Victor Books, 1991).

9. For example, former president Jimmy Carter teaches a Sunday school class for Maranatha Baptist Church in Plains, Georgia. The class attracted 3,700 visitors in 1994, necessitating that the church expand its parking lot. But the attraction is Carter, not Sunday school.

10. Lewis J. Perelman (kanbrain@concentric.net) is executive editor of *Knowledge Inc.*, a newsletter that specializes in "kanbrain" learning (http://www.concentric.net/~kanbrain).

11. For this shift spelled out more completely, see Leadership Network's *NetFax* 34:11 (December 1995). In the realm of Christian education, the shift from training to learning is as follows:

Training	Learning
Goal is knowledge transfer	Goal is obedience/change behavior
Focus on Bible knowledge	Focus on life skills/application
Content/doctrine/beliefs	Felt needs/ministry/maturity
Church based	Home/Community based
Sunday only	Seven-days-a-week
House curriculum only	Best available/House plus others

12. U. S. Department of Education, National Center for Education Statistics, *The Condition of Education* (Washington, D.C.: Government Printing Office, 1993), 30-31.

13. John Wesley, "A Thought on the Manner of Educating Children" (1783) in *The Works of the Rev. John Wesley, A.M.* 3rd ed. (London: John Mason, 1831) 13:436-37.

14. Peter M. Senge, *The Fifth Discipline: The Art and Practice of the Learning Organization* (New York: Doubleday Currency, 1990), 6-10.

15. This phrase is used by Glenn R. Jones, the reigning guru of distance education, in his book *Make All America a School: Mind Extension University, the Education Network* (Englewood: Jones 21st Century, 1991).

16. Richard K. Fenn, *The Secularization of Sin: An Investigation of the Daedalus Complex* (Louisville: Westminster/John Knox, 1991), 188. For a discussion of "God's forgotten language," see Sweet, *Quantum Spirituality*, 217-48.

17. William M. Easum, *Crib Crawl Walk: A Nursery for Our Time* (Port Arkansas: 21st Century Strategies, 1995). Order it from 21st Century Strategies, P.O. Box 549, Port Arkansas, TX 78373.

18. See "The Revolution Begins at Last," *The Economist* 30 (September 1995), 15-16.

19. Charles R. Page, *Jesus and the Land* (Nashville: Abingdon, 1995), 62-66, 99-100, 132-33.

20. For more on ESP, see Patricia A. McLagan and Christo Nel, *The Age of Participation: New Governance for the Workplace and the World* (San Francisco: Berrett-Koehler, 1995), 253-55.

21. William Bridges, *Managing Transitions: Making the Most of Change* (Reading: Addison-Wesley, 1991).

Chapter 9: The CELL Gene

1. John Wesley and Charles Wesley, *Hymns and Sacred Poems* (Bristol: F. Farley, 1742), 83. Selected stanzas can be found in "Jesus, United By Thy Grace," in *The United Methodist Hymnal*, 561.

2. John Wesley, Entry for 1 May 1738, *An Extract of the Rev. John Wesley's Journal from February 1, 1737-8 to His Return from Germany* (London: Printed by W. Strahan, 1740), as reprinted in John Wesley, *Journals and Diaries*, ed. W. Reginald Ward and Richard P. Heitzenrater, vols. 18-23 of *The Works of John Wesley* (Nashville: Abingdon, 1988-1995), 18:236.

3. John Wesley, *The Nature, Design, and General Rules of the United Societies in London, Bristol, King's-wood, and Newcastle-upon-Tyne* (Newcastle-Upon-Tyne: Printed by John Gooding, 1743), 1, as reprinted in John Wesley, *The Methodist Societies: History, Nature, and Design*, ed. Rupert E. Davies, *The Works of John Wesley* (Nashville: Abingdon, 1989), 9:69.

4. John Wesley, *A Plain Account of the People Called Methodists in A Letter to the Rev. Mr. Perronet* (Dublin: S. Powell, 1749) as reprinted in J. Wesley, *The Methodist Societies*, 262.

5. John Wesley, Preface to *Hymns & Sacred Poems* (1739), as reprinted in *The Works of John Wesley* (London: Wesleyan Conference Office, 1872; reprinted Grand Rapids: Zondervan, 1958), 14:321.

6. See John Wesley's 1748 sermon, "Upon Our Lord's Sermon on the Mount Discourse the Fourth," in John Wesley, *Sermons*, ed. Albert C. Outler, vols. 1-4 of the *Works of John Wesley* (Nashville: Abingdon, 1984-1995), 1:533.

7. See Ralph W. Neighbour and Lorna Jenkins, *Where Do We Go From Here?: A Guidebook for Cell Group Churches* (Houston: Touch Publications, 1990).

8. David Hunsicker, "John Wesley: Father of Today's Small Group Concept?" *Wesleyan Theological Journal*, 31 (spring 1996), 192-212. See also David Lowes Watson, *The Early Methodist Class Meeting: Its Origin and Significance* (Nashville: Discipleship Resources, 1985).

9. The best resource is Neighbour and Jenkins, *Where Do We Go From Here?*

10. C. Kirk Hadaway, Francis M. DuBose, and Stuart A. Wright, *Home Cell Groups and House Churches* (Nashville: Broadman, 1987), 42.

11. Quoted in Robert A. Dahl and Edward R. Tufte, *Size and Democracy* (Stanford: Stanford University Press, 1973), 111.

12. John Wesley, Entry for 24 May 1738, in J. Wesley, *Journals and Diaries*, 18:249.

13. Joan R. Gundersen has shown how "the church was literally remade into a home that women proceeded to decorate with their handiwork. . . . Parlors and kitchens were now found in both homes and churches, and women acted as hostesses in these rooms." See her "Women and the Parallel Church: A View from Congregations" in Catherine M. Prelinger, ed., *Episcopal Women: Gender, Spirituality, and Commitment in an American Mainline Denomination* (New York: Oxford University Press, 1992), 111-32. "Congregational facilities themselves began to look like the middle-class homes as parlors, sewing rooms, nurseries, Sunday school rooms, kitchens, dining rooms, and libraries were often added on to pre-existing sanctuaries or were incorporated into new church construction over the course of the nineteenth century."

14. Russell E. Richey "Twins: The Local Church and Denominational Bureaucracy," *Leadership Letters from the Duke Divinity Project on United Methodism* 1 (30 July 1995), 2.

15. Doug Murren, *The Baby Boomerang: Catching the Baby Boomers as They Return to Church* (Ventura: Regal, 1990), 44.

16. Glenn Paauw, "What's So Special About Specialty Bibles?" *Bible Banner* 131 (19 February 1996), 12-15.

17. *The Journal and Letters of Francis Asbury*, ed. J. Manning Potts, Elmer T. Clark, and Jacob S. Payton (Nashville: Abingdon, 1958), 3:253-54.

18. For the strong association of hymns with women before their preeminence in public worship services, see June Hadden Hobbs, "'I Sing For I Cannot Stay Silent': The Feminization of American Hymnody, 1870-1920" (Ph.D. diss., University of Oklahoma, 1994), 85.

19. John Wesley, Entry for 3 July 1766, in *J. Wesley, Journals and Diaries*, 22:48.

20. *Journal of the Rev. Francis Asbury: Bishop of the Methodist Episcopal Church* (New York: N. Bangs and T. Mason, 1821), 1:6.

180

21. John Wesley, "The Character of a Methodist," (Bristol: Felix-Farley, 1742), as found in J. Wesley, *The Methodist Societies*, 41.

22. John Wesley, Entry for 1 April 1739, in J. Wesley, *Journals and Diaries*, 19:46. In Wesley's day, preaching outside the church building was frowned upon by the Church of England. Even as late as 1837 Bishop Samuel Butler wrote: "If the inhabitants will not take the trouble to come . . . far to hear your sermons . . . I am sure they do not deserve to have them brought to their doors" (as quoted in R. A. Soloway, *Prelates and People: Ecclesiastical Thought in England 1783-1852* (London: Routledge & K. Paul, 1969), 341. It wasn't until the 1850s that Anglicans began open-air preaching—going to where the people were.

23. John Wesley, Entry for 1 April 1739, in J. Wesley, *Journals and Diaries*, 19:46. The text Wesley preached from for this field sermon was Luke 4:18-19: "The Spirit of the Lord is upon me, because he hath anointed me to preach the Gospel to the poor. He hath sent me to heal the broken-hearted; to preach deliverance to the captives, and recovery of sight to the blind: to set at liberty them that are bruised, to proclaim the acceptable year of the Lord."

24. *New International Readers' Version: New Testament*, Young Reader's ed. (Grand Rapids: Zondervan, 1995).

25. P. K. McCary, *Rappin' With Jesus: The Good News According to the Four Brothers* (New York: African American Family Press, 1994).

26. For more on this image, see Leonard I. Sweet and Elizabeth Rennie, "The Well that Will Never Run Dry," *Homiletics* 8 (January–March 1996), 39-41.

27. Neal F. McBride, *How to Build a Small Groups Ministry* (Colorado Springs: NavPress, 1995), 15.

28. Russell E. Richey, "Twins," 6.

29. *CellChurch Magazine*, P. O. Box 19888, Houston, TX 77224. Telephone: Touch Outreach Ministries, 1-800-735-5865.

Chapter 8: The STACKING Gene

1. As quoted by David A. Kaplan, "The Force is Still With Him," *Newsweek*, 13 May 1996, 64.

2. Gertrude Stein, *Narrations* (New York: Greenwood, 1968; republication of Chicago: University of Chicago Press, 1935), 34.

3. For a summary statement of the old position, see chapter 3, "One Thing at a Time," in Eknath Easwaran, *Take Your Time: Finding Balance in a Hurried World* (Tomales, CA: Nilgiri Press, 1994), 63-88. For a further discussion of the stacking phenomenon, see Sweet, *Quantum Spirituality*, 268-71.

4. Krauss, *The Physics of Star Trek*, 151.

5. John P. Robinson, "Radio Songs," *American Demographics* 18 (September 1996), 63.

6. R. Laurence Moore, *Selling God: American Religion in the Marketplace of Culture* (New York: Oxford University Press, 1994), esp. 116-17.

7. See Josh Hunt, *Let It Grow: Changing to Multi-Congregation Churches* (Grand Rapids: Baker, 1993).

8. Francis Asbury's address to the General Conference of the Methodist Episcopal Church, May 1816, as found in *The Journals and Letters of Francis Asbury*, 3:532.

9. Francis Asbury to William McKendree, 5 August 1813, as found in *The Journals and Letters of Francis Asbury*, 3:475-76, 478.

10. These ways include linguistic, musical, logical-mathematical, spacial, bodily kinesthetic, and personal. See Howard Gardner, *Frames of Mind: The Theory of Multiple Intelligences* (New York: Basic Books, 1983), 73-276. An excellent resource for Christian educators in telling the stories of the Bible utilizing these seven learning styles is Barbara Bruce, *Seven Ways of Teaching the Bible to Children* (Nashville: Abingdon, 1996).

11. Microtechnology already has produced the Data Link watch, created by Timex and Microsoft working together—it holds phone numbers, alarms, appointments, a to-do list, and two time zones; the Message Watch from Japan's Seiko (800-848-3545) receives radio signals from its own paging service—you also get phone messages, weather forecasts, sports scores, and other information.

12. In the words of MIT professors Nicholas Negroponte and Neil Gershenfeld, "Jewelry that is blind, deaf, and dumb just isn't earning its keep. Let's give cuff links a job that justifies their name." See their "Wearable Computing," *Wired* (December 1995), 256.

13. Sherry Turkle, *Life on the Screen: Identity in the Age of the Internet* (New York: Simon & Schuster, 1995).

14. Leon Wieseltier, "Against Identity," *New Republic* 28 (November 1994), 30.

15. For Alfred Schultz see his "On Multiple Realities," *Philosophy and Phenomenological Research* 5 (1945), 533-76. For Martin E. Marty, see his *The Divinity School in the University: A Distinctive Institution* (Pittsburgh: Association of Theological Schools in the United States and Canada, 1995), 10-11.

16. Marty, *The Divinity School in the University*, 11.

17. Gerard Loughlin, *Telling God's Story: Bible, Church and Narrative Theology* (New York: Cambridge University Press, 1996), 194.

18. Sherry Turkle, as quoted by Pamela McCorduck, "Sex, Lies, and Avatars," *Wired*, April 1996, 164, in an interview discussing her *Life on the Screen*.

19. As quoted in Jeremy Begbie, *Voicing Creation's Praise: Toward a Theology of the Arts* (Edinburgh: T & T Clark, 1991), 211.

20. Tennessee Dixon, *ScruTiny in the Great Round: Interactive Art* (CD-ROM) Santa Monica: Calliope Media, 1995).

Chapter 7: The TEAM Gene

1. Michael Jordan commenting to reporters on why he fed his teammates so many times during the Bulls' thirty-eight-point trouncing of the Orlando Magic in game one of the 1996 NBA Eastern Conference Finals. See Bryan Burwell, "Jordan's Redemption Road Begins as Role Player," *USA Today*, 21 May 1996.

2. M. Mitchell Waldrop, *Complexity: The Emerging Science at the Edge of Order and Chaos* (New York: Simon & Schuster, 1992), 241.

3. Ibid., 241-42.

4. Morris A. Graham and Melvin J. LeBaron, *The Horizontal Revolution: Reengineering Your Organization Through Teams* (San Francisco: Jossey-Bass, 1994).

5. Jon R. Katzenbach and Douglas K. Smith, *The Wisdom of Teams: Creating the High-Performance Organization* (Boston: Harvard Business School Press, 1993), 45.

6. For the various kinds of teams possible, see Susan Albers Mohrman, Susan G. Cohen and Allan M. Mohrman, Jr., *Designing Team-Based Organizations: New Forms for Knowledge Work* (San Francisco: Jossey-Bass, 1995), 40-41.

7. See Leonard I. Sweet and K. Elizabeth Rennie, "Will You Join the Jesus Team," *Homiletics* 8 (January–March, 1996), 27-29.

8. Jessica Lipnack and Jeffrey Stamps, *The Age of the Network: Organizing Principles for the 21st Century* (Essex Junction: Omneo, 1994), 213.

9. Autograph letter of John Wesley to Samuel Walker, 3 September 1756, Maser Wesleyana Collection, Drew University Library, as published in *The Letters of the Rev. John Wesley*, ed. John Telford (London: Epworth, 1931), 3:195.

10. The phrase "collaborative individualism" is that of David Limerick and Bert Cunnington. See their *Managing the New Organization: A Blueprint for Networks and Strategic Alliances* (San Francisco: Jossey-Bass, 1993), 35-36, 112-58.

11. See Andrew J. DuBrin, *The Breakthrough Team Player: Becoming the M.V.P. on Your Workplace Team* (New York: AMACOM, 1995).

12. Thomas Coke, Entry for Sunday, 14 November 1784, *Extracts of the Journal of the Rev. Coke's Five Visits to America*, 16.

13. Penelope Farmer, *Two or the Book of Twins and Doubles: An Autobiographical Anthology* (London: Virago, 1996), 370.

14. Sara Maitland, *A Big-Enough God: A Feminist's Search for a Joyful Theology* (New York: H. Holt, 1995), 5.

15. See for example Michael Goulder, *St. Paul Versus St. Peter: A Tale of Two Missions* (Louisville: Westminster/John Knox, 1995).

16. Henry D. Rack, *Reasonable Enthusiast: John Wesley and the Rise of Methodism* (London: Epworth, 1989; 2nd ed., Nashville: Abingdon, 1993).

17. Doris Elisabett Andrews, "Popular Religion and the Revolution in the Middle Atlantic Ports: The Rise of the Methodists, 1770-1800" (Ph.D. diss., University of Pennsylvania, 1986), 171.

18. Paul Otis Evans, "The Ideology of Inequality: Asbury, Methodism, and Slavery" (Ph.D. diss., Rutgers University, 1981), 231.

19. Randy J. Sparks, *On Jordan's Stormy Banks: Evangelicalism in Mississippi, 1773-1876* (Athens: University of Georgia Press, 1994), 203.

20. Parker J. Palmer, "Community, Conflict, and Ways of Knowing," *Change Magazine* 19 (September/October 1987), 20.

21. See Harvey Robbins and Michael Finley, *Why Teams Don't Work: What Went Wrong and How to Make It Right* (Princeton: Peterson's/Pacesetter Books, 1995).

22. As quoted in Hans J. Eysenck, *Genius: The Natural History of Creativity* (New York: Cambridge University Press, 1995), 1.

23. See for example Eysenck, *Genius*.

24. David Joseph Weeks and Jamie James, *Eccentrics: A Study of Sanity and Strangeness* (New York: Villard, 1995), 16.

25. Nicholas Negroponte, "Where Do New Ideas Come From?" *Wired* (January 1996), 204.

26. Ronald A. Heifetz, *Leadership Without Easy Answers* (Cambridge: Belknap Press of Harvard University Press, 1994), 271.

27. For the fuller story of the National Performance Review, see Lipnack and Stamps, *The Age of the Network*, 129-30.

28. This is a perception of Ross Webber, chair of the management department, Wharton School, University of Pennsylvania, as noted in Brian O'Reilly, "What's Killing the Business School Deans of America?" *Fortune*, 8 August 1994, 65.

29. The Association of United Methodist Schools, *Agenda 21: United Methodist Ministry for a New Century* (S.l.: s.n., 1995), 28.

Chapter 6: The GOOD (Get-Out-of-Doors) Gene

1. Gerard Manley Hopkins, "Inversnaid," *The Poetical Works of Gerard Manley Hopkins*, ed. Norman H. MacKenzie (Oxford: Clarendon, 1990), 168.

2. Michael J. Cohen, "Wilderness Revisited: The Twilight's Last Gleaming" in Cass Adams, ed., *The Soul Unearthed: Celebrating Wildness and Personal Renewal Through Nature* (New York: Jeremy P. Tarcher/Putnam, 1996), 155.

3. See my chapter on Jesus and the out-of-doors in *The Jesus Prescription for a Healthy Life* (Nashville: Abingdon, 1996), 69-85.

4. Wendell Berry is the latest in a long line of writers to point out "how much an outdoor book the Bible is" in "Christianity and the Survival of Creation" in his *Sex, Economy, Freedom, and Community: Eight Essays* (New York: Pantheon, 1993). The Bible "is best read and understood outdoors, and the farther outdoors the better. Or that has been my experience of it. Passages that within walls seem improbable or incredible, outdoors seem merely natural. This is because outdoors we are confronted everywhere with wonders; we see that the miraculous is not extraordinary but the common mode of existence. It is our daily bread. Whoever really has considered the lilies of the field or the birds of the air and pondered the improbability of their existence in this warm world within the cold and empty stellar distances will hardly balk at the turning of water into wine—which was, after all, a very small miracle" (103).

5. J. Ernest Rattenbury, *Wesley's Legacy to the World: Six Studies in the Permanent Values of the Evangelical Revival* (London: Epworth, 1928), 294.

6. As quoted in Norris S. Barratt, *Barratt's Chapel and Methodism* (Wilmington: Historical Society of Delaware, 1911), 8.

7. Thomas Coke, Entry for Sunday, 14 November 1784, *Extracts of the Journals of the Rev. Coke's Five Visits to America*, 15.

8. Lou Gold, "Bald Mountain Vigil" in Adams, ed., *The Soul Unearthed*, 169.

9. As quoted in Simon Schama, "God's First Temples: The Giant Sequoias of Yosemite as the Birthplace of America," *Times Literary Supplement*, 10 March 1995, 16.

10. I thank Rabbi Lawrence Troster of South Orange New Jersey for this insight.

11. John Wesley, "The Danger of Riches," in John Wesley, *Sermons*, ed. Albert Outler, vols. 1–4 of *The Works of John Wesley* (Nashville: Abingdon, 1984–1995), 3:238-39.

12. John Wesley, "The General Deliverance," in J. Wesley, *Sermons*, 2:436-50.

13. Francis Jammes, "mon humble ami," from "L'Eglise Habillée de Feuilles," in his *Clairières dans le Ciel* (Paris: Sociéte du Mercure de France, 1906), 192, with thanks to Mike Clingenpeel, editor of the Virginia Baptist *Religious Herald*, for pointing me to this poem.

14. See for example John Wesley, "The New Creation" in J. Wesley, *Sermons*, 2:500-510.

15. Robert Minhinnick, "The Hot-House," in his *The Looters* (Bridgend: Seren Books, 1989), 23.

16. Fred Krueger, "Why Ecology Is a Christian Issue," *Green Cross: A Christian Environmental Quarterly* (winter 1995), 16-17.

17. John Wesley, "The Use of Money," in J. Wesley, *Sermons*, 2:269.

184

18. John Montague, "A Severed Head," in *The Rough Field* (Winston-Salem: Wake Forest University Press, 1989), 35.

19. As quoted in Suzi Gablik, "A Few Beautifully Made Things," *Common Boundary* (March/April 1995), 41.

20. As reported in *John Naisbitt's Trend Letter*, 30 March 1995, 8.

21. As quoted in Gablik, "A Few Beautifully Made Things," 41.

22. Larry Rasmussen, "The Near Future of Socially Responsible Ministry: Perspectives from Christian Ethics," in Dieter T. Hessel, ed. *Theological Education for Social Ministry* (New York: Pilgrim, 1988), 28.

23. Dieter T. Hessel, "Religion and Ethics to Meet the Environmental Challenge" (paper presented at the Conference on Environmental Values, 1-2 June 1995).

24. *Keeping and Healing the Creation* (Louisville: Committee on Social Witness Policy, Presbyterian Church [USA], 1989); *Restoring Creation for Ecology and Justice*: A Report Adopted by the 202nd General Assembly (Louisville: Office of the General Assembly, The Presbyterian Church [USA], 1990); *Caring for Creation: Vision, Hope and Justice* (Chicago: Evangelical Lutheran Church in America, 1993); *Accelerated Climate Change: Sign of Peril, Test of Faith* (Geneva: World Council of Churches, Program Unit III: Justice, Peace, Creation, 1994).

25. Max Oelschlaeger, *Caring for Creation: An Ecumenical Approach to the Environmental Crisis* (New Haven: Yale University Press, 1994), 212-13.

26. Amy Grant, *House of Love* (Hollywood, A&M Records, 1994), compact disc.

27. To order *The Earth Pledge Book: A Call for Commitment*, compiled and introduced by John F. Ince (Sausalito: Timely Visions Publishing Co.; Gardenia, CA: Distributed by SCB Distributers, 1994), which includes 111 Earth Pledges along with addresses of major environmental organizations and questions from key scientists and environmental leaders, call One World, Inc.: 1-800-Earth95; 415-331-1942; or Fax 415-332-8167 (One World reports faxes may not always go through).

28. Michael J. Cohen, "Wilderness Revisited: The Twilight's Last Gleaming" in Adams, ed., *The Soul Unearthed*, 155-56.

29. Jars of Clay, "Love Song for a Savior," recorded in *Jars of Clay*, 1995.

Chapter 5: The MINISTRY MOBILIZATION Gene

1. Mark Twain, "Extract from Captain Stormfield's Visit to Heaven," in *The Family Mark Twain* (New York: Harper, 1901), 1276. Sandy further explains, "Jones tried heaps of times to enlist as a private, but he had lost both thumbs and a couple of front teeth, and the recruiting sergeant wouldn't pass him. However, as I say, everybody knows, now, what he *would* have been, so they flock by the million to get a glimpse of him. . . . Caesar, and Hannibal, and Alexander, and Napoleon . . . the public hardly care to look at *them* when he is around."

2. Charles Edwin Jones, "The Inverted Shadow of Phoebe Palmer," *Wesleyan Theological Journal* 31 (Fall 1996), 127.

3. Thomas Coke, entry for Sunday 14 November, 1784, *Extracts of the Journals of the Rev. Coke's Five Visits to America*, 16.

4. Don Cupitt, *Radicals and the Future of the Church* (London: SCM, 1989), 138.

5. See among other sources, John S. Simon, *John Wesley and the Methodist Societies* (London: Epworth, 1937), 22-23.

6. Quoted in J. Oswald Sanders, *Spiritual Leadership* (Chicago: Moody, 1967), 69.

7. David L. Smith's *All God's People: A Theology of the Church* (Wheaton: BridgePoint Books, 1996), 354-69, makes the distinction between "fundamental ministry" and "specialized ministry."

8. See Richard Warren, *The Purpose Driven Church: Growth Without Compromising Your Message and Mission* (Grand Rapids: Zondervan, 1995).

9. Michael Slaughter, *Spiritual Entrepreneurs: Six Principles for Risking Renewal* (Nashville: Abingdon, 1995).

10. Carl F. George, *Prepare Your Church for the Future* (Tarrytown: Revell, 1991), 193.

11. Dannie Abse, *Intermittent Journals* (Bridgend: Seren, 1994), 222-23.

12. Leonard I. Sweet, *FaithQuakes*, 33.

13. Mary F. Rousseau, "The Ministry of the Laity," *New Oxford Review* 52 (June 1995), 8-13.

14. Jim Wallis, "Life's Unlimited Value and Our Limited Resources," in J. Robert Nelson, ed., *Life as Liberty, Life as Trust* (Grand Rapids: Eerdmans, 1992), 22.

15. Chuck Lathrop, *A Gentle Presence* (Washington: Appalachian Documentation, 1977), 7.

16. Thanks to Richard Heyduck (Texas Annual Conference) for this analogy.

17. As reported in Guy Kawasaki, *How to Drive Your Competition Crazy: Creating Disruption for Fun and Profit* (New York: Hyperion, 1995), 97.

18. Rowan Williams, *A Ray of Darkness: Sermons and Reflections* (Cambridge: Cowley, 1995), 157.

19. For some sample "position descriptions" which can be adopted and adapted to a variety of ministries in the church, see the Appendix to Brian Kelley Bauknight, *Body Building: Creating a Ministry Team Through Spiritual Gifts* (Nashville: Abingdon, 1996), 101-109. Columbia Baptist Church in Falls Church, Virginia, publishes every year a twenty-page directory of "Ministry Opportunities" that is chock full of ways one can be a minister.

20. Ibid., 33.

21. Brad Johnson, "Innovations for the Disciple-making Congregation," *Growing Disciples* 2 (April-June 1996), 26-27.

22. Bruce Bugbee, "What's Your Servant Profile," *Discipleship Journal* (November/December 1995), 64. See also Bruce Bugbee and Beth Lueders, "Maximum Ministry," *Discipleship Journal* (November/December 1995), 60-62.

23. Peter F. Drucker, Foreword: "Not Enough Generals Were Killed," in Frances Hesselbein, Marshall Goldsmith, Richard Beckhard, eds. *The Leader of the Future: New Visions, Strategies, and Practices for the Next Era* (San Francisco: Jossey-Bass, 1996), xi.

24. Ibid., xi-xii.

25. Jenkins's story is found in David Weeks and Jamie James, *Eccentrics: A Study of Sanity and Strangeness* (New York: Villard, 1995), 89-90.

26. Pope John Paul II, *The Vocation and the Mission of the Lay Faithful in the Church and in the World*, no. 274-78 (Washington, D.C.: Office of Publishing and Promotion Services, United States Catholic Conference, 1989. Also found in "Christifidels Laici: Apostolic Exhortation on the Vocation and Mission of the Lay Faithful in the World," *Origins: NC Documentation Service* 18, no. 35 (9 February 1989), 561-95.

186

27. Bruce Bugbee, *What You Do Best in the Body of Christ: Discover Your Spiritual Gifts, Personal Style, and God-Given Passion* (Grand Rapids: Zondervan, 1995).

28. S. M. Ravi Kanbur, *Poverty and Development: The Human Development Report and the World Development Report, 1990* (Washington, D.C.: World Bank, (1818 H Street NW, Washington, DC 20433), 1991.

29. Susie Stanley, "Empowered Foremothers: Wesleyan/Holiness Women Speak to Today's Christian Feminists," *Wesleyan Theological Journal* 24 (1989), 103-16.

30. Kenneth Kinghorn, "Discovering Your Spiritual Gifts," *Discipleship Journal* (November/December 1995), 54-58.

Chapter 4: The WIRED Gene

1. A. E. Harvey, "The Evidence in Cave 7: Were the Gospels Written Before the Sack of Jerusalem?" *Times Literary Supplement*, 22 March 1996, 6.

2. Eamon Duffy thinks so in *Stripping of the Altars: Traditional Religion in England, c.1400-1580* (New Haven: Yale University Press, 1992), 80.

3. D. W. Bebbington, "Evangelical Christianity and the Enlightenment," in Martyn Eden and David F. Wells, eds., *The Gospel in the Modern World: A Tribute to John Stott* (Downers Grove: InterVarsity, 1991), 66-78.

4. Erik Routley, *The Musical Wesleys* (New York: Oxford University Press, 1968), 32.

5. DeMaria, *Samuel Johnson and the Life of Reading*, 78.

6. John Wesley, *Survey of the Wisdom of God in Creation; or, A Compendium of Natural Philosophy*, 3d. ed.(New York: N. Bangs and T. Mason for the Methodist Episcopal Church, 1823).

7. Charles W. Hargitt, "John Wesley and Science," *Methodist Review* (May 1927), 392. He quotes John Wesley, "Address to the Clergy," in *The Works of the Reverend John Wesley*, 1st American Complete and Standard ed. (New York: T. Mason and G. Lane, 1839), 6:219.

8. Wesley, "Address to the Clergy," 225. See also J. W. Haas, Jr., "John Wesley's Views on Science and Christianity: An Examination of the Charge of Antiscience," *Church History* 63 (1994), 378-92.

9. John Wesley, "The Promise of Understanding," in John Wesley, *Sermons*, 4:283.

10. As quoted in *Wired* (February 1996), 95.

11. Some of the Catholic sites on the World Wide Web include:
Catholic Resources on the Net (http://www.cs.cmu.edu/Web/People/spok/catholic.html)
Christus Rex et Redemptor Mundi (http://www.christusrex.org/)
Catholic Information Center on the Internet (http://www.catholic.net)
Gregorian Chant Home Page (http://www.music.princeton.edu:80/chant-html/)
Catholic Online (http://www.catholic.org/catholic/index.html)
Order of St. Benedict Home Page (http://www.osb.org/osb)
Shroud of Turin Home Page (http://www.cais.com/npacheco/shroud/turin.html)

12. Heather Millar, "The Electronic Scriptorium," *Wired*, August 1996, 94-104, quote on 96.

13. The Monastery of Christ in the Desert's Internet address is http://christdesert.org.

14. Quoted in Millar, "The Electronic Scriptorium," 104.

187

15. See Kevin Maney, *Megamedia Shakeout: The Inside Story of the Leaders and the Losers in the Exploding Communications Industry* (New York: Wiley, 1995), iii, 9-10, especially. Orlando, Florida, is already experiencing CONVERGENCE through a Time Warner project called Full Service Network—turn on your TV and you see a three-dimensional menu—one box labeled movies, another shopping, another sports, another regular TV, another interactive channels (create your own music for the home), another video games (you can play against someone else across town), another education.

16. Arnaud de Borchgrave, "The Bubonic Plague of International Crime," *Insight on the News,* 23 October 1995, 40.

17. Seth Lloyd, as quoted in Charles Platt, "A Million MHz CPU?" *Wired*, March 1995, 125.

18. As quoted in *Current Thoughts & Trends* 11 (October 1995), 28.

19. See "The Revolution Begins, at Last," *Economist*, 30 September–6 October 1995, 15.

20. Ibid.

21. As cited by Nicholas Negroponte, "Bit by Bit, PCS Are Becoming TVS: Or Is It the Other Way Around?," *Wired* (August 1995), 178.

22. Joanna Cole, *The Magic School Bus in the Time of the Dinosaurs* (New York: Scholastic, 1994).

23. See Leonard I. Sweet, "Church Architecture in the 21st Century," *NETFAX* 57 (28 October 1995).

Chapter 3: The HEALTH & HOLINESS Gene

1. Evelyn Waugh, *Vile Bodies* (Boston: Little, Brown, 1930), 301.

2. See Wesley to Robert Carr Brackenbury, 15 September 1790, in *The Letters of the Rev. John Wesley,* ed. John Telford (London: Epworth, 1930), 8:238.

3. Wesley to Charles Wesley, 9 July 1766, *The Letters of the Rev. John Wesley*, 5:20.

4. Essayist Scott Russell Sanders, in his recent collection of essays on "the poetics of space" called *Staying Put: Making a Home in a Restless World* (Boston: Beacon, 1993), has an essay called "Telling the Holy" (145-69), which is inspired by the Apache word for myth (154).

5. Thomas Coke, *Extracts of the Journals of the Rev. Coke's Five Visits to America*, 15.

6. Karl Barth, *The Doctrine of Reconciliation*, vol. 4, bk. 2 of his *Church Dogmatics* (Edinburgh: T & T Clark, 1958), 180.

7. John Wesley, Preface to *Hymns & Sacred Poems* (1739), in *The Works of John Wesley* (Grand Rapids: Zondervan, 1958; reprint of London: Wesleyan Conference Office, 1872), 14:321; where Wesley writes: "The gospel of Christ knows . . . no holiness but social holiness." and "'Faith working by love is the length and breadth and depth and height of Christian perfection."

8. John Wesley, "Sermon on the Mount" (1748), in J. Wesley, *Sermons*, 1: 631.

9. John Wesley, "On Perfection," in J. Wesley, *Sermons*, 3:74.

10. *John Wesley's Letter to a Roman Catholic*, ed. Michael Hurley (London: Geoffrey Chapman, 1968), 56.

11. This is Wesley's own distinctive translation of Galatians 5:6. Where Luther translated it "faith working in love," Wesley translated it "faith filled with the energy of love." See his 1750 sermon, "Catholic Spirit," in J. Wesley, *Sermons* 2:88.

188

12. John Wesley, "Circumcision of the Heart," in J. Wesley, *Sermons*, 1: 402.

13. Marc Ian Barasch, *The Healing Path: A Soul Approach to Illness* (New York: Putnam, 1993), 48.

14. John Wesley, "The Signs of the Times," in J. Wesley, *Sermons*, 2:527.

15. John Wesley, *Instructions for Children* (London: M. Cooper, 1745), 27.

16. Donald W. Dayton, "'Good News to the Poor': The Methodist Experience After Wesley," in M. Douglas Meeks, ed., *The Portion of the Poor: Good News to the Poor in the Wesleyan Tradition* (Nashville: Kingswood, 1995), 65-96, esp. 67-70.

17. Theodore W. Jennings, *Good News to the Poor: John Wesley's Evangelical Economics* (Nashville: Abingdon, 1990), 63, 66, 69.

18. William of Saint Thierry, "On Contemplating God," in *The Works of William St. Thierry* (Shannon: Irish University Press, 1971), 1: 36-37.

19. Richard Allen, *The Life Experience and Gospel Labors of the Rt. Rev. Richard Allen* (Nashville: Abingdon, 1983), 30.

20. Maurice James Quinlon, *Victorian Prelude: A History of English Manners* (New York: Columbia University Press, 1941), 173, as quoted in Michael Hennell, *Sons of the Prophets: Evangelical Leaders of the Victorian Church* (London: SPCK, 1979), 4.

21. See Michael J. Christensen, "Theosis and Sanctification: John Wesley's Reformulation of a Patristic Doctrine," *Wesleyan Theological Journal*, 31 (fall 1996), 71-94; see especially 83.

22. See E. Brooks Holifield, *Health and Medicine in the Methodist Tradition: Journey Toward Wholeness* (New York: Crossroads, 1986); and Leonard I. Sweet, *Health and Medicine in the Evangelical Tradition: "Not by Might nor Power"* (Valley Forge: Trinity Press International, 1994).

23. David L. Larsen, *The Evangelism Mandate: Recovering the Centrality of Gospel Preaching* (Wheaton: Crossway, 1992), 133.

24. Donal O. Clifton and Paula Nelson, *Soar with Your Strengths* (New York: Delacorte, 1992), 17.

25. Until his death in late 1996, Rabbi Edwin H. Friedman was the director of the Center for Family Process, Bethesda, Maryland.

26. Clifton and Nelson, *Soar with Your Strengths*, esp. 9-11. A similar argument targeted directly at the church is made by David S. Young in *A New Heart and a New Spirit: A Plan for Renewing Your Church* (Valley Forge: Judson, 1994).

27. In this I agree with Larry Dossey, *Healing Words: The Power of Prayer and the Practice of Medicine* (San Francisco: Harper, 1993).

28. For a presentation of the positive spirituality of darkness, see my "What Marie Aull Taught Me About the NightLife," *Sweet's SoulCafe*, 2, no. 2-3 (1996). About a spirituality of illness, which tries to remove the stigma from sickness, Susan Sontag says "Illness is the night-side of life, a more onerous citizenship. Everyone who is born holds dual citizenship, in the kingdom of the well and in the kingdom of the sick. Although we prefer to use only the good passport, sooner or later each of us is obliged, at least for a spell, to identify ourselves as citizens of that other place"; *Illness as Metaphor* (New York: Farrar, Straus & Giroux, 1978).

29. My recent book *Health and Medicine in the Evangelical Tradition* helped me work out some of these thoughts from a historical perspective. See also the audio seminar with Rick Warren *The Tides of Change: Riding the Next Wave in Ministry* (Nashville: Abingdon, 1995) as well as *The Jesus Prescription for a Healthy Life*.

30. John Moody, "Safe? You Bet Your Life," *Time*, 24 July 1995, 35.

189

31. Darrell W. Robinson, *Total Church Life: Exalt, Equip, Evangelize*, rev. ed. (Nashville: Braodman and Holman, 1993).

32. John Wesley, "On Patience,"in J. Wesley, *Sermons*, 3:169-79; "The Use of Money," *Sermons*, 2:263-80; "The Good Steward," *Sermons*, 2:281-98.

33. Fred Craddock, "You, Therefore, Must Be Perfect," *Christian Century*, 7-14 February 1990; "You must love without partiality, as God does" (123).

34. Walter Wink, *Engaging the Powers: Discernment and Resistance in a World of Domination* (Minneapolis: Fortress, 1992), 269.

35. Theodore W. Jennings Jr., "Wesley and the Poor: An Agenda for Wesleyans," in Meeks, *The Portion of the Poor*, 21.

36. John Wesley, "On Dress," in J. Wesley, *Sermons*, 3:255.

37. John Wesley, "A Farther Appeal to Men of Reason and Religion, Part 2," in *The Appeals to Men of Reason and Religion and Certain Related Open Letters*, ed. Gerald R. Cragg, vol. 11 of *The Works of John Wesley* (Oxford: Clarendon, 1975), 257.

38. *The Book of Discipline of The United Methodist Church* (Nashville: United Methodist Publishing House, 1996), 59, 63.

39. See S T Kimbrough Jr. and Oliver A. Beckerlegge, eds., *The Unpublished Poetry of Charles Wesley* (Nashville: Kingswood, 1988-1992), 2:298.

Chapter 2: The MUSIC Gene

1. Charles Wesley, "The Inner Life," in *Sacred Poetry: Selected from the Works of the Rev. Charles Wesley*, ed. A lay member of the Protestant Episcopal Church (New York: Episcopal Society for the Promotion of Evangelical Knowledge, 1864), 250.

2. Faith Popcorn and Lys Marigold, *Clicking: 16 Trends to Future Fit Your life, Your Work, and Your Business* (New York: HarperCollins, 1996), 143. "What's different about this awakening is that there's very little agreement on who or what God is, what constitutes worship, and what this ritualistic outpouring means for the future direction of our civilization. After the soul-free 80s, we're busy trying to put passion and meaning back into our everyday lives, to find the old values—faith, hope, charity. We're looking for the essence of ourselves—our lost souls."

3. Peter N. Stearns, *Millennium III, Century XXI: A Retrospective on the Future* (Boulder: Westview, 1996), 176.

4. Douglas John Hall, "The Future of Protestantism in North America," *Theology Today* 52 (January 1996), 464.

5. Dorothee Soelle, "Loving Bach in the World of Torture," in Theodore W. Jennings, Jr. ed., *Text and Logos: the Humanistic Interpretation of the New Testament* (Atlanta: Scholars Press, 1990), 292.

6. Carlton R. Young, *Music of the Heart: John & Charles Wesley on Music and Musicians* (Carol Stream: Hope Publishing Company, 1995), 18.

7. Charles Wesley, "Oh Thou Who Camest from Above," *The United Methodist Hymnal*, 501.

8. S T Kimbrough Jr. "Lyrical Theology," *Journal of Theology* 98 (1994), 18-43.

9. I am appropriating here the terminology of theologian Nelle Morton, who talked about our need to "hear each other into speech." See Nelle Morton, "Beloved Image," and "Hearing to Speech," in *The Journey Is Home* (Boston: Beacon, 1985), 127-29 and 201-221. For a homiletic interpretation of the difference

between hearing and listening, see Leonard I. Sweet and K. Elizabeth Rennie, "Hear the Vision," *Homiletics* 9 (January–March 1997), 13-15..

10. Burt Nanus, "Vision Team," Futurist 30 (May–June 1996), 21, referring to his *Visionary Leadership: Creating a Compelling Sense of Direction for Your Organization* (San Francisco: Jossey-Bass, 1992).

11. Raymond W. Albright, *A History of the Evangelical Church* (Harrisburg: The Evangelical Press, 1945), 35.

12. See the exegesis of the Eli and Samuel text in Sweet and Rennie, "Hear the Vision?".

13. See Joachim-Ernst Berendt's path-breaking book *Nada Brahma: The World Is Sound: Music and the Landscape of Consciousness* (Rochester: Destiny, 1987).

14. Quoted in Peter le Huray and James Day, eds., *Music and Aesthetics in the Eighteenth and Early Nineteenth Centuries* (New York: Cambridge University Press, 1988), 311.

15. Berendt, *Nada Brahma*, 8.

16. Hans Kayser, as quoted in in Berendt, 135-36. "The ears not only recognize exact numerical proportions, that is, numerical quantities like 1:2 as an octave, 2:3 as a fifth, 3:4 as a fourth, etc.; at the same time time they hear . . . values that they perceive as C, G, F, and so on. So the tone value fuses two elements into one unit: the element of sensing—the tone, that is—with the element of thinking, of numerical value. And this happens in such an exact manner that the value of the tone can be checked precisely against the value of the number, and the value of the number against the value of the tone. Among all our human senses, we only have *one* organ that is capable of this fusion: the ears. In this way sensation controls deliberation—or to put it differently: Our soul is thus capable of deciding on the correctness or incorrectness of an intellectual quantity."

17. Michael Talbot, *The Holographic Universe* (New York: HarperCollins, 1992), 51.

18. Rebecca West, *The Fountain Overflows* (New York: Viking, 1956), 14.

19. In case you don't believe me, listen to Max Planck, one of the initiators of quantum physics. As early as 1931 in his book *The Universe in the Light of Modern Physics* he wrote this: "In physics, however, as in every other science, common sense alone is not supreme; there must also be a place for Reason. Further, the mere absence of logical contradiction does not necessarily imply that everything is reasonable. Now reason tells us that if we turn our back upon a so-called object and cease to attend to it, the object still continues to exist. . . . [Such is not necessarily the case.] It is considerations of this kind, and not any logical argument, that compel us to assume the existence of another world of reality behind the world of the senses: a world which has existence independent of man, and which can only be perceived indirectly through the medium of the world of the senses; and by means of certain symbols which our senses allow us to apprehend." (London: Allen & Unwin, 1931), 8, as referenced in Daniel Liederbach, *The Numinous Universe* (New York: Paulist, 1989), 78.

20. Stephen Strauss, *The Sizesaurus* (New York: Kodansha International, 1995), 150.

21. Berendt, *Nada Brahma*, 59, 76-77.

22. "Vibration is undoubtedly part of the creative force of the cosmos; pulsars, snowflakes, and hydrogen atoms vibrate, filling the universe with scin-

tillant radiation." Chet Raymo, *The Virgin and the Mousetrap: Essays in Search of the Soul of Science* (New York: Viking, 1991), 156.

23. Charles Wesley, "Praise the Lord Who Reigns Above," *The United Methodist Hymnal*, 96.

24. Berendt, *Nada Brahma*, 40.

25. Johann Kepler, *Epitome of Copernican Astronomy and Harmonies of the World*, trans. Charles Glenn Wallis (Amherst: Prometheus Books, 1995), 200.

26. Emily Dickinson, "This World is not Conclusion," in *The Complete Poems of Emily Dickinson*, ed. Thomas H. Johnson (Boston: Little, Brown, 1924), 60.

27. J. S. Eades, "Dimensions of Meaning: Western Music and the Anthropological Study of Symbolism" in J. Davis, ed., *Religious Organization and Religious Experience* (New York: Academic Press, 1982), 195.

28. W. A. Mathieu's *The Musical Life: Reflections on What It Is and How to Live It* (Boston: Shambhala, 1994), where he argues that "music makes an altar out of our ears" (215).

29. I wish to thank Dr. Virginia Hoch for helping me develop this christological analogy of perfect pitch.

30. Carl Zimmer, "First Cell," *Discover the World of Science*, November 1995, 71, describes David Deamer's process: "taking the pattern of nucleotides in DNA (ACGT) and substituting E for T he turned them into meditative melodies." Deamer's *DNA Music* is available in cassette form from Science and the Arts, P.O. Box 428, Aptos, CA 95001. The cost, as of this printing, is $12.00 plus $2.00 postage and handling. Their web page: http://vll.com.SusaA/. Their e-mail address: xjander@got.net.

31. See Mary Catherine Bateson, *Composing a Life* (New York: Atlantic Monthly Press, 1989), 1.

32. Joseph Lanza, *Elevator Music: A Surreal History of Muzak, Easy Listening, and Other Moodsong* (New York: St. Martin's Press, 1994).

33. Maltbee D. Babcock, "This Is My Father's World," *The United Methodist Hymnal*, 144.

34. Except for "There's a Church Within US, O Lord," *Hymns for the Living Church* (Carol Stream: Hope Publishing Company, 1978), 208, all numbers are from *The United Methodist Hymnal*.

Chapter 1: The ALTARS-GATE Gene

1. I want to thank Thomas O'Donnell of New Hartford, New York, for the phrase "Altars-Gate."

2. John Wesley, Preface to *Hymns and Sacred Poems* (1739), as found in *The Works of John Wesley* (Grand Rapids: Zondervan, 1958), 14:321.

3. George F. Will, "A Moral Environment for the Poor," *The Washington Post*, 30 May 1991, A19. No written documentation is available to support statements attributed to Roger Starr.

4. Fred Barnes, "Washington Diarist: Up Against the Mall," *The New Republic*, 21 October 1991, 43.